Simon J. Allison

Brexit – a Betrayal of Conservatism?

Copyright © 2018 by Simon Allison

All rights reserved. No part of this publication may be reproduced, distributed, or transmitted in any form or by any means, including photocopying, recording, or other electronic or mechanical methods, without the prior written permission of the author, except in the case of brief quotations embodied in critical reviews and certain other noncommercial uses permitted by copyright law.

About the author

Born in August 1965, Simon Allison grew up in the North-West London and South Hertfordshire suburbs. After securing a first-class history degree from Oxford University, he has worked in finance and the hotel sector before founding a small business. He fought the seat of Croydon North for the Conservatives in 2001. While he has published a number of pamphlets, leaflets and articles in both the business and political arenas, this is his first book.

"When bad men combine, the good must associate; else they will fall, one by one, an unpitied sacrifice in a contemptible struggle"

[Usually paraphrased rather more pithily as "The only thing necessary for the triumph of evil is for good men to do nothing"]

British philosopher, Edmund Burke, considered by many to be the intellectual founder of Conservatism

"First they came for the socialists, and I did not speak out—because I was not a socialist. Then they came for the trade unionists, and I did not speak out— because I was not a trade unionist. Then they came for the Jews, and I did not speak out—because I was not a Jew. Then they came for me—and there was no one left to speak for me."

Pastor Martin Niemöller, German opponent of Hitler who died in a concentration camp two weeks before the end of World War II, having at first welcomed the Third Reich

Contents

Chapter 1 – Introduction ... 1

Chapter 2 – The Conservative Party's Problem ... 7

Chapter 3 – What does a real British Conservative believe? ... 15

Chapter 4 – Does Brexit make the UK more, or less, secure? ... 19

Chapter 5 – Does Brexit support the wealth creators in the country? ... 39

Chapter 6 – Will Brexit assist the government in pursuing a prudent spending policy? ... 71

Chapter 7 – Will Brexit help to preserve the United Kingdom? ... 101

Chapter 8 – Does Brexit help the Rule of Law; and the maintenance of law and order? ... 111

Chapter 9 – And what about Sovereignty? ... 117

Chapter 10 – Conclusions – Is Brexit Conservative? ... 127

Chapter 11 – A truly Tory U-turn ... 139

1. Introduction

Most political books are written either by politicians, academics or journalists. I am none of those and, as a result, some readers may wonder what makes me qualified to put down the thoughts contained herein. The answer is twofold – both political and personal.

On the political front, I am writing it because nobody else has done so – a truly extraordinary situation when there are around four million Conservative voters who backed (and who mostly still back) a policy of remaining in the European Union but who have been abandoned almost entirely by their elected representatives.

For the vast majority of those voters, who have to abide by at least a minimal set of business ethics in their daily lives, the distortions and scare tactics, outright lies and criminal cheating on financial matters which were central to the Leave campaign, mean that the squeakingly narrow victory of that faction is not morally legitimate. They see it as reasonable to ask searching questions of a government committed to a hard form of Brexit (especially as the Brexit process unravels further with each succeeding week), and perhaps also justifiable to stand up and argue that the status quo offers a far better option for the UK than either hard ("poverty") or soft ("poodle") Brexit.

BREXIT – A BETRAYAL OF CONSERVATISM?

On a personal level my life has followed as Thatcherite a playbook as it is possible to design. I was born into a family which had no long-term ties to the Conservatives (my father having been a Young Liberal constituency chairman and my mother having voted Labour in the early 1950s). My parents had turned firmly against the Socialists when their bungalow in North London was compulsorily purchased by Labour to make way for the notorious Chalk Hill estate, which became one of the most deprived high-rise slums in the country and much of which was demolished in 2000, though not before it had helped transform Brent from a Conservative into a Labour area (long before the Westminster "homes for votes" scandal). There was no market price mechanism in those days so my parents were paid only land value – and that only after a long residents' campaign – and had to move to a two storey house, something that was not great for my mother who had recently suffered from heart failure, probably triggered by the scarlet fever she had contracted as a girl. As a result of all this, I grew up in a house where the Labour Party was loathed and feared, where my parents were in tears in 1974 when the election results came in and where my mother would regale us with stories of the trade union "closed shop" at IPC magazines which meant that the entire company would come out on strike if she changed the lightbulb on her desk, because only members of the Electricians Union could change a lightbulb!

The Labour Party cemented its bogeyman status for

CHAPTER 1

us later in 1974 when I got into a direct grant school – only for the new government immediately to take the grant away, forcing us to pay full fees.

I grew up as committed a Conservative as it is possible to be, flying the Union Jack out of my bedroom window during the Falklands War and putting a poster of Maggie on my teenage wall.

To repay my parents' faith in me, I secured a place at Oxford, whose Freshers' Fair in October 1984 was the only thing preventing me being in the Conference hotel for the Brighton bombing. Before starting at university I had become a Young Conservative Constituency Chairman and used my "year off" to work as a Library Boy (junior researcher) at Conservative Central Office, where the other two entrants were Robert Peel (great, great, great nephew or something similar of the nineteenth century PM, Robert Peel) and Ed Llewellyn (who went on to be David Cameron's Chief of Staff).

Then off to university where my course of study was termed "Modern History" but, this being Oxford, that covered the years from 476 to 1914. Nonetheless, it was a very useful introduction to geopolitics, the creation of England and then the UK and to how our foreign policy throughout history has been focused on preventing Europe from uniting against us.

From Oxford I went into the City, and from there to my best client, a fund that owned hotels. In 2001, I fought Croydon North for the Conservatives and went on to reach four final selections for the 2005 elections in highly winnable seats. The Tories took three of them but sadly I had missed out. Instead, like adventurers from the seventeenth to the nineteenth century, I went east to work, did quite well as an expat and then returned in 2013, having set up my own business.

Oxbridge graduate, banker, Tory candidate, corporate executive and then entrepreneur – as I noted above, a very Conservative life.

So much for the bio. Who cares? Why is any of that relevant?

Because if somebody with my deeply ingrained Tory background feels increasingly sidelined and vilified in the modern Conservative party, it is hard to see where it is headed. Nonetheless, today I am one of many active and committed Conservatives who now find themselves outcasts in many Tory circles, one of those activists who still nurtures the policies on which the Party fought – and usually won – elections from 1979 to 2015: pro-business, assertively internationalist, strong on standing up to Russia, in favour of free trade especially with our European partners, on the side of fiscal prudence, willing to spend on defence and the police, cautiously progressive.

It was a policy mix which was balanced but with an ability to be radical; confident; and able to appeal beyond the old, white middle- and upper-class bastions of Conservatism to the aspirant working class and to ethnic and other minorities. It was a winner.

Today, it lies discarded by the roadside. The Conservative Party is populist and isolationist, less focused on making Britain prosper than it has ever been during my lifetime. Its activist base has taken over the party and has itself been taken over in many constituencies by UKIP supporters and other hard-liners.

The struggle to keep the Conservative Party united, somehow to bind together its moderate and pro-European wing with its nationalist and isolationist one has been going on since the early 1990s, with the party leadership continually tacking to the Eurosceptic right to appease its hard-line critics. That attempt has been a failure. We have not bought ourselves "peace with honour". The divisions within Conservatism are now gulfs perhaps too wide to bridge. Some moderates feel more in common with Chukka Umunna's Labour vision than with their own party's policies on trade or foreign policy; at the same time, the European Research Group sounds entirely like the parliamentary wing of UKIP.

People like me are now having to ask – did I get it all wrong? Were our glory years just a mistake? Is Toryism really a hard-right, populist, anti-European sect; or is it actually time to stand up and fight for the beliefs we hold dear?

Let us make no mistake – Britain's place in the world and the future security and prosperity of our children is at stake. Brexit is not a mild change of direction – it represents the turning away from a generation of policy-making and from any aspirations whatsoever that we may have to determine the direction of the Continent in which we must, perforce, live; and indeed to ensure that our Continent can stand united in the face of the long-term challenges posed by renewed aggression from Russia and the rise of the Asian giants.

So one has to ask – is it us, the moderate pro-Europeans who are on the wrong side of history? Or is Brexit a dead-end from which the only sensible escape is a rapid turnaround?

The coming pages will examine that question.

2. The Conservative Party's Problem

When Jeremy Corbyn was elected Labour leader, promoting the kind of far-left agenda not seen since the Foot/Benn days of the 1980s, Britain pretty much knew what to expect. We could expect to look forward to:

· Attacks on the main financial institutions which underpin capitalism, like the Treasury, the Bank of England and the IMF;

· Blistering criticism of British business and especially its leaders; and the espousal of policies to make their lives much harder;

· Excuses being made for Vladimir Putin, even for his invasion of Ukraine and annexation of the Crimea;

· A willingness to sacrifice the Unions with Scotland and Northern Ireland if they stood in the way of ideological purity; indeed, a flirting with policies which could create a united Ireland, something of which Corbyn has long been a supporter;

· Attacks on the bastions of the British constitution like our independent judiciary and the House of Lords for any decisions which looked as if they were seeking to maintain the status quo;

and indeed, over the last three years we've had all of that. But not only – or even primarily – from Corbyn. Those points, *all of them outlined above*, came from the Conservative benches during the Referendum and since then, in many cases, even from the Government.

The Tories have started to sound like the Far Left.

For many Conservative voters, particularly those from the ABC1 social classes (basically, the middle class) and those with higher levels of education – i.e. those people who have comprised the backbone of Tory electoral support for a century – such developments have been shocking.

Those voters have consequently abandoned the Conservative Party in droves, as the loss in 2017 of seats like Kensington, Oxford West, Lincoln, Canterbury, Bath, Stroud, Enfield North and Battersea illustrates all too clearly. Other normally safe seats like Chipping Barnet and Putney were converted into marginals.

At that election, Labour was ahead of the Conservatives *among graduate voters* by 49% to 32% – a lead of 17%.

When Margaret Thatcher took on the Foot/Benn opposition in 1983, the result was a majority for her of 144; Theresa May, the next female PM of the UK, taking on a similarly "unelectable" left-wing opponent, fell 14 seats short of any majority at all.

Given that Labour is also stuck in the hands of its

own extremists and led by a far-left leader who was disowned by 75% of his MPs before the 2017 poll and whose unwillingness to condemn terrorism by enemies of the West is only matched by his unwillingness to maintain proper UK defences, the Tories should be miles ahead of Labour, but they are not. As of September 2018, Labour actually had a poll lead of 4%, despite the unsavoury nature of Mr Corbyn becoming more apparent daily and deep splits within Labour.[1]

Where has it all gone so horribly wrong for the Conservative Party?

The answer lies in a single word – Brexit.

Brexit is the logical conclusion of the growth of Euroscepticism across the grassroots of the party membership, supported by a dedicated and resolute group of MPs with hard-line views. However, there is no indication that this trend has brought greater electability. Since the Conservative Party has adopted Euroscepticism in the mid-1990s, *it has secured a majority at only one out of six general elections*. In contrast, from the late 1960s up to 1992, when it was the most pro-European of the main parties, it won majorities at *five out of seven*.

Today, Brexit has not only exacerbated the divisions within the Conservatives to the point where there is far greater enmity between some pro- and anti-EU Tory MPs than between Conservative MPs and those of other parties, but it has also pushed aside almost anything else in the potential legislative agenda. Nor, as the only real policy currently on offer, is it a startling success; each week brings new hurdles, new complexities and new humiliations, while the promises of the Leave campaign crumble into dust:

· There is no £350 million per week for the NHS. There never was – the UK pays less than half of that to the EU. Instead, we face paying £39 billion to meet our financial obligations to the EU, without even the certainty that such a payment will allow us to keep full access to the EU market

· With NHS staff from the EU leaving in increasing numbers – and they made up 10% of all NHS doctors and nurses in 2016 – our health service faces its biggest ever crisis. Brexit adds to the massive pressure on the NHS.

· There is no prospect of Turkey joining the EU and flooding us with immigrants as we were told. In contrast to that claim, British business now faces labour shortages, meaning either bankruptcies or an inward rush of non-EU citizens who want to work here, who will inevitably come in significant numbers from Asia and Africa, who will inevitably prove in some cases to be more difficult to integrate into British society. The latest immigration figures bear that out, showing a considerable reduction in the pace of arrivals from the EU and an increase in arrivals from Africa and Asia.

· Liam Fox's claim that a trade deal with the EU will be "one of the easiest in human history" is unravelling each day – as is the idea that "they need us more than we need them". Theresa May now makes it clear that Brexit involves lots of hard choices; choices which, at the time of writing, the Cabinet has agreed to resolve with the fudged "Chequers" proposal which has upset both wings of the Party and has anyway, for the most part, been rejected by the EU.

Against that background, there is no massive public endorsement of the government's path, no sense that No 10 is responding to an overwhelming national demand. In fact, *remaining* in the EU has enjoyed an overall opinion poll lead for the last eight months, a lead which is now widening.

So, stepping back from the Westminster bubble, any neutral commentator would have a right to ask why the government so stubbornly clings to policy that is now opposed by majority opinion, is alienating its core voters, is likely to bring at least short-term economic pain, is swallowing almost the entire Parliamentary timetable to the detriment of every other problem which needs tackling and is proving almost impossible to implement.

(In contrast, when the issues with the Poll Tax became clear, the Major government eventually consigned it to the dustbin of history and saved the 1992 election as a result).

BREXIT – A BETRAYAL OF CONSERVATISM?

The answer lies in the almost religious fervour with which Brexit is regarded among a small but pretty fanatical coterie of MPs and a large swathe of the Conservative Party membership (which of course selects – and potentially deselects – the MPs and also makes the final decision in any contested leadership contest).

For them, and perhaps for many unquestioning right-wing activists, it has become axiomatic that you cannot be a Conservative and still support EU membership. Indeed, they like to portray backing Remain as an unpatriotic act, something which nobody who sees themselves as a citizen of the UK, rather than a citizen of the world, could ever seriously contemplate. In late July 2018 one Tory backbencher, ex-UKIPper David Campbell-Bannerman, even suggested that anyone with "extreme EU loyalty" should be tried for treason.

Just as Theresa May has decreed that anyone voting Leave "must have" wanted to leave the Single Market and the Customs Union, for which there is no evidence at all (actually, polls suggest that a significant majority wanted to stay in the Single Market); just as the National Front at one time hijacked the English flag; so equally the Brextremists have hijacked patriotism and Conservatism, and declared anyone who does not agree with them an apostate.

Even pro-European Conservative MPs in today's Parliament, with only a handful of brave exceptions, pay lip service to the "will of the people", ignoring the lies and cheating of the Leave campaign and the fact that the polls have turned, and arguing – against their real beliefs – that Brexit is inevitable and instead of being opposed must only be softened.

Hang on a minute though.

Around four million voters who backed the Conservatives in 2015 went on to vote Remain (42% of all Tory voters). Indeed, even after the Referendum it was estimated that around 3.5–4.0 million Tory voters in 2017 were Remainers and a Survation Poll commissioned by pressure group Citizens for Britain and published in the Independent bore that out.[2]

A majority of Conservative MPs in 2016 also backed the Remain side as did the current Prime Minister. Certainly, the vast majority of politicians associated with the glory days of 1979–1992 are passionate Remainers – people like John Major, Michael Heseltine, Ken Clarke, Chris Patten and Douglas Hurd.

Are none of these real Conservatives? What then is a true Conservative? And with the Party split down the middle, might they actually be the carriers of the flame rather than the UKIP-inspired fanatics of the hard-right?

It's time to take a look.

3. What does a true British Conservative believe?

The "Conservative and Unionist Party" (which for the purposes of this tome includes its predecessors, the Conservative Party and before them the Tory Party) has, in many policy areas, adopted a confusing array of contradictory ideas over time.

It has been passionately in favour of free trade and also passionately protectionist; it has backed appeasement and voted for war; it has been authoritarian, paternalist and libertarian, occasionally at one and the same time; it has encouraged immigration and discouraged it; it legalised the trade unions and then legally constrained them; it has been internationalist and isolationist, elitist and meritocratic, socially liberal and socially conservative.

Anyone trying to draw a simple conclusion about what the Conservative Party really believes in, across a wide range of policies, will come unstuck.

However, there is a core of beliefs which <u>does</u> run right through the Party's history, unchanging and fundamental, for over two hundred years. They could be summarised as:

1) Keeping the country secure from foreign enemies

2) Supporting the wealth creators in the country, ranging originally from the landowners when farming was the country's main economic activity, through to industry and now to the technology and service sectors – in the firm belief that if wealth creators can succeed and generate jobs, there will be economic security for everyone in society

3) Maintaining a sensible and balanced fiscal policy, combined where possible with the lowest reasonable level of taxation

4) Belief in preserving the Unions with Scotland and (now Northern) Ireland

5) Maintenance of the rule of law; and of law and order internally

6) Support for the Monarchy

While there are always a few exceptions which prove the rule, like the handful of Libertarian right-wingers who would like to see the UK as a republic (or possibly as part of the USA), for most of its history, the vast majority of Conservative voters, members and MPs have supported those six policies, regardless of the other issues the country has faced or other divisions within the party.

Sometimes, of course, even these core beliefs have faced internal contradictions. Stanley Baldwin and then Neville Chamberlain, for example, in tackling the economic troubles of the 1920s and 30s by reducing

CHAPTER 3

government spending, tried to adopt an isolationist foreign policy stance and cut defence spending to the bone, with the unfortunate side effect of encouraging Hitler's ambitions, leaving him safe in the knowledge that the UK did not have the money or inclination to stand up to him. (One might argue that today's defence cuts are having a similar effect on Vladimir Putin).

Or you can look at 1914 when the desire to prevent Home Rule for Ireland (a passion more-or-less equal to the Brexit fanaticism of today) led the Conservatives to back an army mutiny and challenge the rule of law.

Generally, however, the combination of core policies outlined above have been self-reinforcing. A country which is kept secure by well-equipped armed forces, where the rule of law means that it is safe to invest and where a strong police force can ensure public peace, is usually a prosperous country. Prosperous countries can in turn fund care for the needy, education for our children and the necessary armed forces to keep the country safe, so creating a virtuous circle.

Does Brexit fit that mould? Does it reinforce that virtuous circle? Is it really what Conservatives should support?

Leaving the monarchy where it would firmly wish to be, well out of this debate, let us look at the other five policy areas one at a time.

- Does Brexit make the country more, or less, secure?

- Does Brexit support the wealth creators in the country?

- Will Brexit assist the government is pursuing a prudent spending policy ensuring job creation and maintaining a tax base which allows the government to provide the key services our citizens have a right to expect?

- Does Brexit strengthen, or weaken, the two critical Unions which hold our country together, those with Scotland and Northern Ireland?

- Is Brexit conducive to the Rule of Law and will it help or hinder the maintenance of law and order?

Only once we know the answer to those questions, can we truly judge whether Conservatives with an inclination to stay in the EU can legitimately oppose it or whether they need to buckle up and accept the ride.

Let's tackle them one by one.

4. Does Brexit make the UK more, or less, secure?

For as long as we have existed as a nation, it has been the fundamental foreign policy objective of Britain – and before then of England – to ensure that the Continent of Europe could not be united against us. Indeed, one might argue that it's really the only foreign policy we have ever had.

None other than Boris Johnson summed this up very neatly, as quoted from his first "out" article prepared for the Referendum result in Tim Shipman's excellent book, All Out War.[3]

"We have spent 500 years trying to stop continental European powers uniting against us".

On that, at least, he was right. It is the reason we fought the Armada, Louis XIV, Napoleon, the Kaiser and Hitler and the reason we founded NATO and stood up to Soviet Russia.

Everything else we've done in our history, everything else we've achieved, has been subordinated to that fundamental and existential aim.

The rationale behind this unchanging objective is quite simple. The nearest point in Europe (leaving aside Ireland) is just 20.7 miles (33.3 km) away. The distance to the nearest point in North America is 3,656 miles (5,883 km) or 176 times further. While Continental Drift may gradually pull us towards the Americas, it is likely to take a few hundred million years which, with apologies to Harold Wilson, is a long time in politics.

So, Europe is the continent where, for good or ill, we are stuck.

The Brexiteers would argue that it doesn't really matter because:

1) We are an island, so not part of the Continent

2) Our glory came from our global empire, both in terms of trade and conquest – Europe is merely a distraction

3) Instead, we are better off pursuing "splendid isolation"; we can be a new Singapore

None of this stands up to scrutiny.

1) Are we an integral part of Europe?

Historically, the answer is a resounding "yes" at almost any level. Ethnically, the vast majority of the UK population originated on the Continent, whether their blood descends from Celts, Romans, Angles, Saxons or Jutes, Vikings, Normans, or more recently French Huguenots, Dutch Protestants, Jews fleeing Russian pogroms or Nazi genocide or Poles and Romanians settling over the last 20 years.

CHAPTER 4

Our royal family is essentially of foreign origin, today having a large element of German blood. Indeed, the monarchs under whom some of our most famous victories were won did not even speak English as their main language, like French-speaking Richard the Lionheart whose statue sits outside Parliament, or German-speaking George I and II (the latter of whom was the last king to lead our forces into battle, at the 1743 Dettingen victory over the French).

Above all, nearly all of British history involves (whether we approve of that or not) a massive amount of involvement in or with the Continent. Richard I's cousin, for example, was elected Holy Roman Emperor. We ruled parts of France from 1066-1558, a far longer period than the UK has existed. We were in a Union with the Kingdom of Hanover for 123 years. Winston Churchill, fearing France's surrender in 1940 offered a "complete and indissoluble Union" with France – and he is regarded as the epitome of patriotism not just for Conservatives but for pretty much everyone else too.

Europe has also been the key element in British prosperity over the years, whether that involved exports of Cornish tin to the Roman empire, the medieval wool trade, the sale of products of the industrial revolution or, more recently exports of cars made at Nissan's Sunderland plant.

We may be an island but we are an island at the edge of a massively important continent; it is not a fate from which we can escape. Moreover, there is no other

Continent of which we can claim membership – the UK is not African or American or Australasian; it is European as a matter of geographical fact and no referendum vote can change that.

2) Did our glory and prosperity come from the Empire?

There is no question that the growth of the British Empires from 1700 – 1783 and again from 1800-1939 became the mainstay of our global power and our self-image, especially for those on the political centre-right for most of whom the Empire is a source of pride not shame. Regardless of political leaning, many schoolchildren will have been taught at least something about victories at Plassey and Quebec; James Cook's discovery of Australia; Gordon's heroic defeat in Khartoum; and equally about the loss of the Thirteen Colonies, the disastrous retreat from Kabul and the siege of Mafeking.

The Eurosceptic rhetoric would tell you that a "Blue Water" strategy, which involved turning our backs on Europe and heading out to open water was what made Britain great. It sounds plausible. After all, Queen Mary's loss of our last Continental possession, Calais, in 1558 came only a few years before her sister and successor, Elizabeth I unleashed her pirates across the Atlantic and began the tradition of English and later British naval victories.

Unfortunately, that all rather disguises the fact that

CHAPTER 4

Britain's expansion was determined almost entirely by what happened on the Continent. Setting fire to the Armada's ships while they were holed up in Flanders (now on the France/Belgium border near Dunkirk) is what kept Britain safe in 1588 along with alliances with Protestant states like the Netherlands and some German principalities, and later with France, against the might of Imperial Spain.

The centrality of what happens on the Continent to the fate of England, and then of the UK, has remained true over time.

For example, looking forward to the real start of Britain's imperial momentum in the seventeenth century, there were wars where we did quite well but our European allies didn't, like the War of the Austrian Succession. In those cases we gained little or nothing in the way of colonies. Equally, there were wars where our allies did extremely well, like Frederick the Great in the Seven Years' War and then we were able to keep our colonial gains.

The biggest setback the Empire ever faced, the loss of the American "Thirteen Colonies" in 1783, was not (apologies to our friends across the pond) mainly due to the gallantry of George Washington, but rather to the intervention of the French and Spanish navies which helped to cut off British forces and ensure their surrender at Yorktown – an act of revenge for Britain's superlative successes during the Seven Years' War. (If it is any consolation, the American War bankrupted

France and was a major factor in the French revolution, giving us yet another chance to indulge in our national hobby at that time of crushing them in war, this time against Napoleon).

That war, too, focuses us on the importance of what happened in Europe rather than in the far-flung Empire. It was victories at Trafalgar (off the Spanish coast) and Waterloo (now in Belgium) which secured our defeat of Napoleon; and his crazy invasion of Russia which fatally weakened him, not – for example – our seizure of Sri Lanka or islands in the Caribbean. Our main armies and the bulk of our navy were generally kept for use on the European front, because an invasion from France would overturn all the good work done by our colonial armies.

Simply put, the history of Britain shows that we didn't fight European wars in order to gain an Empire; we gained an Empire as a by-product of winning wars in Europe (or rather, generally, of paying other people to win them for us) and we focused on the Empire as a source of strength to back our struggles for mastery in Europe, providing both men and materiel.

So much for conquest – what about trade?

The isolationists will also tell you that our prosperity as well as our greatness was built on trade with the Empire but sadly, that is not quite right either: By 1820, 30% of Britain's exports went to its Empire, rising slowly to 35% by 1910.[4]

CHAPTER 4

Even at the peak of Empire, the largest share of our exports went to Europe.[5]

The policy of Imperial Preference i.e. of imposing tariffs on non-Empire goods but not on those of British colonies and dominions, much revered by Joseph Chamberlain, boosted UK exports to the Commonwealth slightly, or possibly merely slowed their decline, but pushed up food costs and was extremely unpopular – being blamed for Conservative electoral defeats in 1906 and 1910, again in 1923 and finally in 1929.

The two World Wars of course disrupted historical trends, with the UK having to rely much more on its Empire and on the USA, but overall it was a short-lived period. Looking forward some decades, one of the reasons we joined the EU was because trade patterns were already, by 1970, reverting to historical norms, with Europe gradually replacing the dominance of the Commonwealth and the USA. In 1960, among the UK's top ten export markets for goods, the USA, Canada, Australia, India, New Zealand and South Africa made up 34% of all such exports; by 1970, only the USA, Australia, South Africa and Canada remained in the top ten, with their share down to 24%. In 1960, of the then EEC nations, only Germany and the Netherlands were in our 10 top export markets, together taking 8% – while by 1970, they had been joined by the Netherlands, France and Belgium/Luxembourg taking 19%.[6] In other words, joining the EEC wasn't the cause of a rebalancing of our trade away from the

Commonwealth and into Europe – it was a result of it, though of course by ending preference for goods from the Commonwealth, it undoubtedly hastened the trend thereafter

Today, among non-European countries, only the USA and China are in the UK's top ten export markets, taking just under 20%.[7] We have reverted to our usual trading pattern whereby it is Europe which generates our prosperity, not far-flung nations.

The idea that our wealth depended on the Empire/Commonwealth rather than Europe and could do so again, does not wash.

3) But even then, "splendid isolation" was better, wasn't it?

Brexiteers like to hark back to a mythical golden age in which Britain was free of foreign entanglements.

In truth, the UK has rarely sought, or experienced, true isolation. Indeed, as part of the key foreign policy aim of preventing Europe from being united against us, we have generally been in alliance with one great power or another – Burgundy against the French in the fifteenth century; France and the Netherlands against Spain in the sixteenth; France against the Netherlands and then – confusingly – the Netherlands against Louis XIV's France in the seventeenth; Prussia, Russia or Austria against France in the eighteenth and early nineteenth; France and Turkey against Russia in the Crimea; France and Russia against Germany during

CHAPTER 4

the two World Wars; Germany, the USA and France against Russia after 1945.

So true isolation has been rare and, when it occurred, it was neither desirable nor splendid at all. In the last hundred and twenty years, we have seen two periods when we tried to turn our backs on Europe. The first ran from the late nineteenth century up to 1914 (a bit of a clue that) or, more properly, up to 1902. It's worth exploring that one a little more as it tells us a great deal about what being truly isolated feels like. (The second, which we shall tackle later, finished in 1939, which is a bit of a clue too.)

In the late nineteenth century, Britain felt no need of alliances. Our Empire was vast, our Queen was also Empress of India, our navy maintained the two-power standard which meant that it insisted upon being bigger than the next two navies in the world combined. (At the start of World War I we had 400 ocean-going warships; we have 19 today). We were on top of the world; allies were not a necessity. In 1898 we won perhaps Britain's greatest strategic victory in a little-known place called Fashoda when a British force trying to link our African Empire from north to south met a French one trying to unite its possessions from East to West. The result wasn't a battle but a climbdown by France, abandoning its key strategic objective when faced with the prospect of taking on mighty Britain. Winning a war might bring greatness – but winning it just by threatening to fight it is surely a sign of greatness already achieved, of an Empire truly at its zenith.

Then, just a year later, it all went wrong. The UK found itself engaged in a nasty local war with the Boer settlers in South Africa which resulted in unexpected setbacks and British retaliation including the creation of the world's first concentration camps to keep Boer families away from their fighters. Global reaction was universally hostile. Every other nation saw us as a bully and there was sabre rattling from across Europe. Britain realised that it was utterly alone.

Suddenly the Empire looked vulnerable. Even a two-power naval standard would not allow you to fight a coalition of all the other major powers in the world. Memories were stirred of Napoleon's Continental System (an attempt in the early nineteenth century to exclude the UK from all European markets) and the Leagues of Armed Neutrality (1780-83 and 1800-01) whereby all the main navies of Europe united to prevent intrusive inspections by the Royal Navy.

Britain needed a solution and that meant allies not isolation. In retrospect, the path we chose was exactly the wrong one – instead of focusing on the key imperative of keeping the balance of power in Europe, we instead sought to preserve the balance of power elsewhere in order to preserve the Empire, first signing an alliance with Japan to contain Russian ambitions in the Far East and then settling our colonial disputes with France and subsequently with Russia itself, in the form of a

CHAPTER 4

non-aggression pact called the Triple Entente which developed into an "almost-alliance".

A bit like the Chequers White Paper of July 2018, it was a compromise position nobody had planned, nobody really wanted and the implications of which nobody properly understood. The Entente was intended to forestall wars with Russia in Asia or France in Africa and South-East Asia. It was not intended to become a military alliance in Europe. However, as relations warmed with our new partners, they cooled with Germany whose aspiration to create a world-class navy did not go down well in Whitehall. Assumptions began to be made about how the UK would behave if a general European war broke out. The Entente meant that when war was looming in 1914, France was encouraged to be belligerent because they were sure the UK would get involved; and Germany was encouraged to be belligerent because they were confident we would not. By pretending to ourselves that we were not really involved in what happened on the Continent, we failed to prepare for the forthcoming disaster and failed to foresee it. Instead of driving a European solution of our own, we messed around on the sidelines and then got sucked in anyway because, of course, we could not allow Germany to crush the French and dominate Europe.

Of course that is not how history got written. Britain's entry to the Great War was portrayed as a principled stand to defend the sovereignty of "plucky little

Belgium" but, although that played a major part in steeling a wobbly Liberal cabinet to declare war, it was not the key strategic consideration. The fundamental military imperative was based on the fact that, under the Entente, the French had redeployed their navy to the Mediterranean leaving the Royal Navy to defend the North Sea. If we didn't act, those vital channel ports i.e. Antwerp, Dunkirk, Calais, Boulogne – whose control had always mattered to Britain – would fall to the powerful German Navy. It could not be allowed.

Had the UK made that clear at the outset, German policy might have been different. But by pretending that we weren't truly involved in the struggle for mastery in Europe, we ended up getting drawn in anyway to defend our vital national interests.

Not for the last time, our attempt to be "not really part of Europe" ended in tragedy.

After the mess of World War I, we again tried to turn our backs on Europe and again found that we couldn't. The Baldwin and Chamberlain governments of the 1930s pursued an isolationist policy that was fervently supported by the vast majority of Conservative members and activists, who shunned the brave anti-appeasement stances of Churchill, Eden and Macmillan. A certain Mr Hitler had other ideas and we were at it again. Trying to wish away the importance of our own backyard and attempting to balance the country's books by ignoring its strategic interests were policies

CHAPTER 4

which directly contributed to the onset of World War II – an entirely avoidable catastrophe.

It is worth pausing a moment to highlight the very stark similarities between the situation in the late 1930s and those of today. The era of the strongman was very much to the fore with authoritarian, populist leaders in Hungary, Poland and Italy and the rise of the far-right in Germany (mercifully, with far less success more recently than back then). The liberal democracies were weak and unable to hold onto the global structures upon which they relied to keep the peace, especially with America turning its back on the world and Mussolini successfully defying the League of Nations to intervene over Italy's invasion of Abyssinia. Russia hovered menacingly to the East. In the UK, however, the government, recovering from a deep economic downturn, was enjoying the peace dividend by reducing our armed forces dramatically and had entirely lost the plot in terms of Britain's geopolitical role, thinking that "a quarrel in a faraway country between people of whom we know nothing" would not impact greatly on the UK.

Sadly for Chamberlain, the fundamental logic of Britain's geographical position meant that even if we did not want to get sucked into events on the Continent, in the end we had no choice – and we started from a far worse position than if we had faced up to the reality of our proximity in the first place.

And then after 1945, having finally learnt the lessons

of 1914 and 1945, the looming Russian threat brought Britain into NATO primarily to prevent a Russian conquest of Europe. As so often in the past, we pushed our military frontier well away from our borders, the better to protect them. It was a policy wholeheartedly supported by the Conservative Party and, at least as of now, still is.

What all of this tells us is that isolation just isn't possible or desirable, whether we like it or not. Even the supposed architect of "splendid isolation", the great Lord Salisbury himself, eventually recognised the futility of it.

"There is all the difference in the world", he noted, "between good natured, good humoured effort to keep well with your neighbours, and that spirit of haughty and sullen 'isolation' which has been dignified by the name of 'non-intervention'. We are part of the community of Europe and we must do our duty as such".[8]

Where does this quick historical overview that leave us?

- With the knowledge that we are an integral part of the European story, that it has always been the mainstay of our economic prosperity and that attempts at isolation did not make us richer, or safer or more glorious.

- With the realisation that Europe is too important to be left to the French and the Germans to run, possibly in ways that run counter to our interests.

· And with the understanding that the key military victories which created our greatness were almost without exception won on the Continent of Europe.

Today's threats to British security

Would we repeat such victories today? In a globalising world, of course we face new threats from a resurgent Russia run by a thoroughly unpleasant cabal of ex-KGB hacks intermingled with state-sponsored gangsters, quite prepared to commit murder on British soil; from Islamic extremism; and, in the long-run from an increasingly wealthy and fast-militarising China.

These are threats not just to Britain but to the entire Western World and they are threats of a magnitude which can only be tackled jointly.

Take Putin's Russia with which the new populist right seems to have a strange love affair – to the extent that, at the 2016 Party Conference, John Redwood could be heard at a fringe meeting claiming that Putin had been forced to invade the Ukraine due to the EU's provocation (which is a bit like arguing that poor old Hitler had been massively provoked by those aggressive Czechs).

(If you're not up to speed on what the ardent Brextremists think about Vladimir Putin, take a look at a video called *Someone Had Blunder'd* in which they essentially defend his invasion of the Ukraine as a reaction to an evil EU plot!).[9]

Russia today has not gone the way the West hoped it would after the collapse of the Soviet Union. It is returning to the Cold War days of being a hostile militarised state, not afraid to use hard power to invade Georgia and the Ukraine or to prop up the mass murderer Bashir Assad in Syria.

Putin boasts openly about his military build-up and his apparently new and invincible nuclear weapons. Russian planes and submarines now fly aggressive sorties in the North Sea. To ignore this threat would be extremely foolish; but it seems that Britain currently has a Prime Minister who questions whether we need to be a Tier 1 military power – a far, far cry from the Iron Lady days of Margaret Thatcher.

At the same time, we are seeing Russia attempt to sow discord in the West and to divide the Europeans and Americans from each other, both between and within countries. We know that Russia funds the French National Front; we know it interfered massively in the US Presidential election to assist Donald Trump and that he now repays the favour by trusting Putin more than the FBI. Russia also cosies up to hard-line nationalist parties in Italy, Poland and Hungary. We have no definite proof of course that Russia bankrolled the Brexit campaign, whatever the balance of probabilities, but for sure anything which drives a wedge between the UK and our NATO allies is a massive benefit to the Russian drive for renewed superpower status.

This is not just theoretical but a highly topical issue.

CHAPTER 4

Since we cannot fight Russia on our own (and a war between Russia and NATO would be a catastrophe) it seems that our main weapons are economic; indeed, sanctions have been used quite successfully against the Putin regime for years. However, if the UK is outside the EU, it will be far harder to persuade the Europeans to enact sanctions for our benefit and sanctions by the UK alone would not have much leverage. Moreover, the UK has often needed to work quite hard to stiffen the backbone of countries like Germany which depend heavily on Russian energy supplies – if we are no longer at the table, a flabbier response may be expected, leaving us isolated and the West divided. With Donald Trump increasingly questioning the basis for NATO and perhaps putting into doubt America's commitment to defend Europe from Russia, it could hardly be more vital that the European nations are bound closely together.

Of course, the Brexiteers will argue that NATO is the defensive alliance and that it has nothing to do with the EU. While that's strictly true in a legal sense, it ignores a whole raft of policy areas where the UK's membership of the EU has been an important part of our security – data sharing, foreign policy, closer defence co-operation, procurement and arms exports, UK roles in EU missions, diplomatic support in the event of isolated attacks like Skripal, how European defence policy develops and whether it remains NATO-linked or not etc. For the UK to be outside the EU just as the EU beefs up its defence capabilities is to abdicate the responsibility for the security of our continent – just as we did in the 1930s. It is not just about weapons; it is also about policy.

The West is being challenged as never before. Neutral countries are increasingly beguiled by the perceived strength of unelected leaders; and neutral states run by corrupt Presidents – which is most of them – find China's willingness to overlook human rights violations and rigged elections most attractive. As we lose our global economic leadership, so the basic freedoms we espouse are also coming under concerted challenge from around the world. A period of 500 years when Europe expanded eastwards taking its ideas, its liberalism and its concepts of honesty and decency with it (even if we did not always adhere to them ourselves) is ending. The next 500 years will see us continually on the retreat – our populations and our economies of increasingly little importance. The West – which geopolitically means Europe, the USA, Canada, Japan and Australia/New Zealand -must hang together. Anything which cracks our unity will threaten our demise. Whatever fluff the isolationists put around it, Brexit threatens that unity. It weakens the West and weakens our influence within the West. It therefore weakens the realm. That is the opposite course to what any Conservative should support.

So much for soft power i.e. how the UK exerts its influence. Let us turn to the harder stuff and how

CHAPTER 4

Brexit impacts not just geopolitics but our armed forces themselves.

It is amazing to look back over the past thirty years and see how badly our defences have been run down, by Conservative governments pursuing austerity as much as by Labour governments which are weak on patriotism. Today, our army numbers 77,000 (over 4,000 short of its target of 82,000 and too small to fill Wembley Stadium); and actually that is probably a bit optimistic – apparently, as reported in the Sunday Express, 20% of British armed forces are not classed as "medically fully deployable".[10]

In simple terms, we can no longer afford to defend ourselves, as general after general has warned.

That cuts across what most Conservatives would see as the most fundamental duty of any government – defence of the realm. As anyone who has read Paul Kennedy's fabulous tome *The Rise and Fall of the Great Powers* knows, in the end to be a powerful military nation, you have to have the necessary financial resources.[11] No money, no army.

Given that our armed forces are already pared back to the bone, our security depends on making the country more prosperous so that we have some capacity to build them back up again. Does Brexit do that? Let's turn to the next chapter to find out.

5. Does Brexit support the wealth creators in the country?

Firstly, let's make it clear that by wealth-creators, I do not just mean big business, but also the entire infrastructure of competitiveness on which the UK's future economic success depends. Thus, the term encompasses entrepreneurs, directors and employees of small businesses, financiers, scientists, technicians, farmers and teachers.

While the eventual impact of Brexit has been much discussed, it is perhaps worth considering for a moment what all of these groups, who will have to work with the on-the-ground implications of Brexit, think about it.

At the time of the Referendum, the CBI had compiled a summary of the findings of all the main business groupings. Its own members favoured remaining in the EU by 80% to 5%; the slightly more Eurosceptic Institute of Directors by 63% to 29% and the even more anti-EU British Chambers of Commerce by 54% to 37%. Tech UK was pro-Remain by 70% to 15%.

At the other end of the spectrum, the Trades Union Congress, the famous TUC, bête-noir of the Heath and Thatcher governments and historically not a friend of the EU, was also pro-Remain and is today campaigning to remain in the Single Market.

As for teachers, a poll published on 17th June 2016 showed that teachers planned to vote Remain by 73% to 26%; while staff in higher education supported Remain by 89% to 9%.[12, 13]

In a survey of financiers, support for Remain was 67% to 25%.[14]

So, even if Brexit *might* support our wealth creators, it is clear that the opposite does not apply – overwhelmingly, business, unions, financiers and educators in our society were in favour of EU membership.

Economists, with the exception of hardened Brextremists, also predicted dire results for the UK from a Leave vote and yet, for most people, two years on nothing terrible seems to have happened, which has led the Brexiteers to claim it was all Project Fear. Were these experts simply wrong, as Michael Gove liked to boast?

It is a cheap and perhaps easy shot to dismiss all of these people as the "liberal elite". In reality, they are the people who are most likely to understand the complexities of Single Markets, Customs Unions and trade treaties. So why did they back staying in when a clear majority of the rest of Britain voted to leave? What do they know that others do not?

Let's start by dismantling the myths of complexity and bafflement that all these trade-related terms tend to cause. Some of what follows may be criticised by purists, but hopefully it simplifies the main essence of what we are talking about.

CHAPTER 5

Customs Union – this is a combination of different countries which eliminate trade taxes (mainly called tariffs) between them, but then have a common tariff policy with the rest of the world. The original "Common Market", which we joined in 1973, was exactly that. The way it works is that the countries in this Customs Union can buy and sell from each other without the need to pay taxes on imports and exports on goods going in and out and have no need to worry about where all the parts come from in a completed product if they all originated in the EU. However, any goods or services from outside that Customs Union, when they arrive, will be taxed at the same – agreed – rate by all the countries within it. For obvious reasons, countries within a Customs Union cannot then go and negotiate separate trade deals with the same countries that the Customs Union has signed treaties with or the whole system would collapse.

Single Market – this is a big extension of the Customs Union whereby a whole range of obstacles to trade between the different countries within it get dismantled. You may think that if the tariffs on internal trade have disappeared there are no obstacles left, but that's far from the case. Different regulations (especially safety and other standards) and varying professional qualifications could stop you exporting (say) beer to Germany or setting up an accountancy practice there. The Single Market was designed to get rid of most of these so-called "non-tariff barriers" which often made trade between countries, especially in services, almost impossible (and remember that tariffs make trade more expensive but they do not prohibit it so in many ways non-tariff barriers are a more serious problem).

WTO – The World Trade Organisation is the regulatory boy which sets standards and monitors disputes between countries or customs unions i.e. it would rule on a trade dispute between the USA and the EU or between Japan and China but not between countries within the EU. Countries can of course have trade deals between each other (bilateral trade deals) but if these do not exist, trade is governed by WTO rules and these will usually have a varying level of tariffs depending on the products concerned, for example 10% on automotive parts up to 40% on some agricultural products.

If you listen to the Brextremists today, they will tell you that we only signed up to a Common Market in 1972, that nobody had any idea it would end up with a political construct and that the British people have been pulled blindly down a path to a Federal Europe by (either) Socialist plotters or integrationist Europeans.

Like so much of their propaganda, it is simply not true.

Firstly, the 1975 Referendum on European Membership, won by the Remain side 2:1, was very definitely fought on the basis that staying in the EEC would have political consequences. Here is a leaflet from the 1975 No campaign, which makes that explicitly clear:

CHAPTER 5

> **Britain a mere province of the Common Market?** The real aim of the Market is, of course, to become one single country in which Britain would be reduced to a mere province. The plan is to have a Common Market Parliament by 1978 or shortly thereafter. Laws would be passed by that Parliament which would be binding on our country. No Parliament elected by the British people could change those laws.
>
> This may be acceptable to some Continental countries. In recent times, they have been ruled by dictators, or defeated or occupied. They are more used to abandoning their political institutions than we are.
>
> Unless you want to be ruled more and more by a Continental Parliament in which Britain would be in a small minority, you should vote NO.

(NO Campaign Leaflet, 1975)[15]

Of course, people didn't vote "NO". The Yes campaign was led by a certain Margaret Thatcher and she won a resounding victory.

Margaret Thatcher in 1975: Conservatives say yes to Europe
(©: ZUMAPRESS.COM/Keystone Pictures USA/age footstock)[16]

And a decade after that sweeping victory, Mrs T signed the Single European Act, the very measure which created the Single Market. Why did she do that? Was she defeated in Parliament? No. Was she bludgeoned by nasty foreigners? No again. Instead, the creation of the Single Market was the flagship European project of the Thatcher governments, a means to sweep away all the tricks by which other EU countries could stop us exporting to them or sending our professionals to work in their countries. It was a triumph for advocates of open markets, forced through in the face of resistance from a reluctant France.

So, what went wrong?

As we know, the British tend to have a respect for rules which some other European countries, especially those further south, may not always share. In order to make the Single Market work, we all agreed that a neutral "referee" would be needed to enforce the rules. As the Single Market was an EU project, so the EU would provide that referee. At the start, that seemed a great idea; but then, at some point, we realised that we would not always get the verdict we wanted – sometimes, we would lose; and very occasionally we have.

For the Brexiteers, that is an appalling diminution of sovereignty (a subject we shall discuss at length later). The idea that we might be overruled in the European Court of Justice, or have regulations decided over our objections by the votes of a majority of EU countries, was anathema to them and still is.

CHAPTER 5

The problem in this, as in any system which brings together people, companies or countries, is that there is always a referee – without one, nothing gets done. If we were to leave the EU and trade under WTO rules, then, as Wikipedia explains:

> *By joining the WTO, member countries have agreed that if they believe fellow members are in violation of trade rules, they will use the multilateral system of settling disputes instead of taking action unilaterally — this entails abiding by agreed procedures (Dispute Settlement Understanding) and respecting judgments, primarily of the Dispute Settlement Body (DSB), the WTO organ responsible for adjudication of disputes. A former WTO Director-General characterized the WTO dispute settlement system as «the most active international adjudicative mechanism in the world today.*[17]

Unlike the European Court of Justice ("ECJ"), the DSB is not "our" court, abiding by rules we have made as one of the EU's leaders; instead, we would be under the WTO rules, a body in which our voice is smaller. Consequently, leaving the EU wouldn't make us entirely free from external courts and while we would in theory be freer to ignore the WTO, in practice we would not do so. We are too dependent on trade to become a pariah nation, too vulnerable to retaliation if the rules-based system were to collapse.

Perhaps the narrative has run on too far, too fast– let

us go back to what it means to leave the Single Market and the Customs Union.

If Britain leaves the Single Market, we are no longer part of the system of mutual recognition of standards and qualifications. We also step away from the other elements which, over time, have become integral to the Single Market – free movement of people (actually workers), capital, services and goods, a contribution to the economics (i.e. costs) of making the system work and an acceptance that the EU sets the market's rules by majority vote and that the ECJ enforces it.

If we leave the Customs Union as well as the Single Market, we no longer have the benefit of the trade treaties the EU has negotiated with other countries, but at the same time, we would be free to sign trade deals of our own.

For a lot of Brexit voters, this once sounded great. No more contribution to the EU budget, no more "undemocratic" EU rules, no more ECJ jurisdiction – what could be better that that? We can, they argue, go back to the days of Drake and Clive, roaming the blue oceans and trading with whomsoever we want. Control would be truly taken back!! It was this romantic vision which was sold to Leave voters and which they bought into.

If only it were so easy.

There are really a lot of problems with this "blue ocean" strategy and the main ones are:

CHAPTER 5

1) We still need to trade with the EU; it is by far our biggest market and outside the Single Market we would over time encounter the same non-tariff barriers that existed before we drive through the Single Market project. Or, if we want to keep full access to that Market from outside the EU, we would probably still need to pay into the budget, abide by the EU's regulations (but not get to make them), accept the four freedoms including free movement of workers, and be subject, on disputes related to the Single Market, to the judgements of the ECJ. Or we could be less closely involved and accept a less-than-full access – but only if the EU agreed to that, which so far it shows no signs of doing. The indivisibility of the four freedoms has been set as the fundamental red line which Michel Barnier, the EU's chief negotiator, has been told not to cross.

2) If we were also to leave the Customs Union, we would lose the benefit of the trade treaties which the EU has already concluded, after literally years of hard bargaining, with 52 other countries such as Canada, South Korea, South Africa, Mexico, Israel, Egypt etc; we would almost certainly lose free access to EU markets for our service industries which make up around 80% of the UK economy; and we would need to start again negotiating trade deals for ourselves.

This is the crux of the current heated debates about

what sort of Brexit we want. The menu on offer tends to be portrayed as:

· Norway/Switzerland option – Under this, we would keep access to the Single market, obey its rules, contribute to it to a greater or lesser degree. This has nuances. Norway, Switzerland, Iceland and Liechtenstein are part of The European Free Trade Association ("EFTA"), an intergovernmental organisation which looks to promote free trade but does not create a customs union and is not a body with a political element (in contrast to the EU). Separately, three out of the four EFTA members (but not Switzerland) are part of the European Economic Area ("EEA") along with all the EU countries. All EEA countries adopt the EU's Single Market rules as well as a lot of other regulations in areas like the environment, company law and consumer protection but not agriculture or fisheries policies. To be in the EEA you have to be either in the EU or in EFTA.

· Canada Option – We would leave the Single Market (i.e. the need to keep identical regulations but also the benefits from doing so); we may pay something for access to tariff-free access to EU markets; we lose the existing trade treaties but are free to make our own

· Bespoke deal – we could try to get the best of both worlds by getting largely free access to the EU markets while still leaving both the Customs Union and the Single Market. At the time of writing, the government has created a fascinating mish-mash of a policy in a White Paper which we will discuss shortly.

· We could Remain in the Customs Union but leave the Single Market

· Finally, we could remain in the EU and so, by definition, in both the Customs Union and the Single Market.

How does all this complexity result from a deal we were told was going to be so simple? Indeed, why did Brexiteers ever think it was going to be simple at all? They seem to have convinced themselves that because we have a "traded goods deficit" with the EU (in plain English, they sell more "stuff" to us than we sell to them), they therefore need us more than we need them – because their companies and their jobs depend on exports to the UK – and so they will have no choice but to give the UK a great deal.

It is true that the UK imports more from the EU than it exports. As the excellent (neutral) website Full Fact notes, "Exports of goods and services to other EU countries were worth £240 billion in 2016, while exports from the rest of the EU to the UK were worth about £320 billion."[18]

Germany has the biggest trade deficit with the UK of over £25 billion and that is why Brexiteers pinned their hopes on the German car industry in pushing hard to stop any trade barriers with the UK.

However, that is not the whole story. From a negotiating perspective, of far more importance is that the UK sends around 43% of all its exports to the EU; while the EU sends only 8% of its exports to the UK. Looked at another way, as Full Fact put it:

> *The £240 billion exports of goods and services to other EU countries were worth about 12% of the value of the British economy in 2016. It's been at around 12-15% over the past decade.*
>
> *Exports from the rest of the EU to the UK were worth about 3-4% of the size of the remaining EU's economy in 2015.*[19]

If you are wondering why the UK doesn't seem to be doing very well in the negotiations with the EU, it is down to those stark facts.

Not only is the EU economy much bigger than the UK's, but we also depend on selling to the EU far more than the EU as a whole, or any country within it, depends on selling to us.

Cutting ourselves off from EU markets just is not viable and so we have recognised that we are going to have to make concessions in order to retain that market access.

Some of the Brextremists just don't buy that, especially the boisterous Boris. They will claim:

1) The rest of the world wants to do deals with us, especially the USA, India and China and that will make up for any lost trade with the EU. (Donald Trump enjoys building up our hopes in that direction).

2) EU bureaucracy is holding us back and we would do far better as a nimble and flexible country outside it.

3) Trade with the EU anyway is a shrinking proportion of our trade, as the rest of the world surges ahead – we are currently "tied to a corpse".

Let's deal with those arguments one at a time:

a) The world is gasping for the opportunity to do deals with the UK which will rescue us

If the UK leaves the EU with no trade deal, or a rather poor one, and especially if it has to revert to WTO rules, we will urgently need to replace the lost trade with the EU and also with those other 52 countries which have signed deals with the EU, because those deals would all lapse at the same time. The UK will be in an astonishingly weak position; we will be desperate for new trade deals and, funnily enough, when you are desperate your negotiating position isn't too hot. *Can* we do such deals? Sure! Will they be good for us? Perhaps not. As we are finding out from our current negotiations with the EU when you are on the back foot, you tend to have to make a lot of concessions. India, for example wants the UK to open up more immigration as part of a trade deal – we are likely to have to concede that. China is one of the toughest negotiating parties out there, not exactly hindered by being the world's most dynamic economy; it will be fun negotiating intellectual property protections in that treaty!

And of course that leaves our supposed saviour, Donald Trump.

If you have not been following world affairs, you will perhaps have missed Donald Trump's speeches berating his predecessors for being too harsh with America's trading partners, demanding that the US lower tariffs across the board and insisting that his diplomats sign the draft Trans-Pacific Partnership as soon as possible. Oh, sorry, that was just a dream, one of Liam Fox's I think.

Anyone who reads the papers will know that Trump tore up the TPP almost immediately, is successfully renegotiating NAFTA (the North American Free Trade Area) with Canada and Mexico to America's advantage, tried unsuccessfully to impose tariffs of 292% on Anglo-Canadian aircraft manufacturer Bombardier and has just slapped 25% tariffs on imported metals. He is the most protectionist US President since the War and while he may love to thumb his nose at the EU by suggesting he will put the UK at the front of the queue in trade talks, the most likely scenario is that he's not going to do Britain any favours at all. Chlorinated chicken is the least of our problems.

CHAPTER 5

In sum, relying on Trump to save Britain with a good trade deal is like booking the Pope to do your bar mitzvah! It ain't gonna happen.

What is more, even if it did, it wouldn't be enough. Leaving aside the Brextremist rhetoric, *The Economist* magazine took a look at the UK's exports to the EU and related countries like Norway and Switzerland and found that they were 2.6x the size of our exports to the USA.[20]

So if leaving the EU were to see a 10% fall in exports, we would need to increase exports to the USA by 26% to make up for it. And that is just the revenue line. Selling into the US is likely to be more expensive due to higher transport costs and the need to adapt products for new standards. So maybe we would actually need to increase sales by 30-40% for British companies to get the same profits and be able to employ the same number of people at the same wages. (That leaves aside the need to compete in an aggressive environment where the courts are far from even-handed; just ask BP – many UK companies have found a somewhat uneven playing field when they went into American markets).

Moreover, aside from the particulars of US, Chinese and Indian government policies and regulations and even setting aside the weakness of our negotiating position, the idea that long-distance trade will easily replace our trade with Europe is challenged by a fundamental of global trade economics which Economics Online describes as follows: "The gravity model suggests that relative economic size attracts countries to trade with each other while greater distances weaken the attractiveness".[21]

Basically, the model says that as you double the distance between two economies, the amount of trade between them reduces (and in some examples, halves).

When you think about that, you don't have to be a scientist or economist to realise how likely that is to be true. It's not just about transport costs, of course. There is also the problem of communicating across distant time zones; vastly different concepts of contract law, negotiation style and, culturally, of how business works; and the higher risk of entering unfamiliar markets where competitors are less well understood.

In simple terms, selling to a customer in France may involve a two-hour journey on Eurostar, a conversation in slightly broken English and the cost of a container from (say) Stoke to Lyons. Any problems, you can always pick up the phone. Selling the same item in China involves a long-haul flight, probably an interpreter, and a very lengthy transport route. The rule of law is not going to protect you if anything goes wrong; and if you want to call, you'd better get up early. And of course, a competitor in (say) Vietnam, quite possibly ethnically Chinese herself and able to converse in Mandarin, can probably undercut your price.

So, perhaps the brave new world of international trade is not going to be as rosy as it has been painted. Saying that isn't "doing Britain down" any more than a football pundit predicting we were not going to win the 2018 World Cup was "doing Britain down". It is just a case of facing reality.

But at least, the Brextremists would argue, it is surely better than being bound to the EU with its endless bureaucratic rules and an inability to secure trade deals of our own.

b) A nimble UK will do better alone

The Brexiteers are definitely convinced that rather than relying on the EU, we should do trade deals "ourselves, alone" or to give that phrase its Irish translation, "Sinn Fein". The Tory Party's Sinn Feiners are convinced that if we negotiate on our own, without having to satisfy the needs of 27 other countries, we can boost our trade quickly and easily. To some extent, they do have a point (actually it is one of their better points). The EU is undoubtedly hamstrung by needing to carry all 28 nations and several regional assemblies with them every time they do a trade deal. The recent Canada-EU Comprehensive Economic Trade Agreement (mercifully, CETA for short) was seven years in the making, only minimally includes services and agricultural products and has over 1,000 pages of exceptions, but despite all that effort it was nearly derailed by the regional Parliament of Wallonia, a part of Belgium – and the new isolationist government in Italy is, even now, threatening to veto it.

Once the UK trains up a new cadre of trade negotiators (after 40 years of the EU doing it for us, we barely have any of our own) we will, for sure, be nimbler.

How much nimbler is hard to say. Even without the need to satisfy Spanish fishermen, French farmers, German IT engineers and Italian fashion houses, cutting trade deals is really arduous. The table below shows how long it took the USA to negotiate and implement its own trade deals:

Time taken to negotiate US Free Trade Agreements (months)

Country	Time from beginning of negotiation to implementation
Jordan	18
Australia	22
Israel	29
Bahrain	30
Mexico	31
Canada	32
Morocco	35
Chile	36
Dominican Republic	37
El Salvador	37
Singapore	37
Honduras	38

Nicaragua	38
Guatemala	40
Oman	45
Peru	56
South Korea	69
Costa Rica	71
Colombia	96
Panama	102
Average	**45**

(Calculated using data from the Office of the United States Trade Representative)[22]

From launch date to implementation, the average time was four years and while some advanced economies were quicker (like Australia and Singapore) others like South Korea were slower.

Moreover, speed of execution is not the key to getting good trade deals. That comes down to pure power. Big countries, with more to offer and more to threaten, will get better deals than smaller countries. Our negotiating strength today is as part of the world's largest single market and largest integrated economy, a prosperous block of 512 million people. On our own, we are just 66 million; it's not the same. One can hardly stress too often that doing a deal is not the same as doing a good deal (as Theresa May is currently discovering).

c) At least we won't be "tied to a corpse"

This was one of the great myths of the Leave campaign, that the EU was a collapsing economy, that the Euro would dissolve and that the Greek financial crisis would bankrupt the whole shooting match. Well, it hasn't happened. The Euro is still around and the EU economy is now growing at 2.5% versus the UK's at 1.8%.

Nor has the supposed dead hand of EU bureaucracy held everyone back. Website tradingeconomics.com shows the value in US$ of Britain's and Germany's exports to three key markets:

· The USA – the home of our "special relationship" and a key part of the Anglosphere

· China – the world's most dynamic major economy

· India – the fastest growing population in absolute terms and of course linked to the UK by language and history:

Destination of exports	Exports by Germany (US$ billion) [23]	Exports by the UK (US$ billion)[24]
USA	118	62
China	85	18
India	11	4

Germany, exporting twice as much to the USA, nearly three times as much to India and nearly five times as much to China, doesn't seem to be hampered too much by EU regulations. If our trade balance is rather poor, the problem may not lie in Brussels …

It is also worth noting that the other countries in the supposed "Anglosphere" may not be quite as convinced of its unique value as the Brexiteers claim; indeed, the idea that they are diplomatically tied into us in some glorious post-colonial bond of loyalty is just fanciful. As Gideon Rachman notes in his excellent book *Easternisation*, "An internal exercise by Britain's Foreign Office in 2014 found that India voted against the British position at the UN more often than any other large nation".[25]

What about the argument that the EU is just old and slow and that our exports with the rest of the world are growing much faster and that will solve the problem? As with so much of what the Leavers argue, it has an element of truth but misses the key point. Yes, emerging markets are indeed growing faster than EU economies and also faster than the UK economy. That is because they are *emerging* markets, starting off from a low base and so being able to accelerate faster as they industrialise. Britain being inside or outside the EU does not change that and a Britain outside the EU will be a less attractive treaty counterparty for these nations than a Britain inside the EU.

As for the Commonwealth being a keen supporter of the UK leaping into "freedom" it is a bit strange that key heads of state of the main Commonwealth nations all recommended a Remain vote in 2016!

Malcolm Turnbull, the then Australian PM said:

> *The EU is an enormous economic and political entity and from our point of view – you might say from our selfish point of view – having a country to whom we have close ties and such strong relationships is definitely an advantage. So if the British people, in their wisdom, decide to stay in the European Union, then we would welcome that......Britain's involvement in the European Union does provide us – and Australian firms particularly, many of whom are based in the UK – considerable access to that market. From our point of view it is an unalloyed plus for Britain to remain in the EU.*[26]

Meanwhile, the Indian Prime Minister Narendra Modi said that the U.K. is India's *"gateway to Europe.... India always stands in support of a strong and united Europe."*[27]

Canadian PM Justin Trudeau agreed, noting *"Britain is always going to have clout, it's just obviously amplified by its strength as part of the EU"*.[28]

Looking at all of this evidence, it is rather difficult to conclude that British trade will benefit from leaving the EU. Certainly, exporting our way out of a slump in trade to our former European partners by seeking markets in the rest of the world seems to be something of an illusion.

In the end, as the government has reluctantly realised, certainly in the short-term and maybe in the longer-term too, we have no option but to secure tariff-free access to EU markets – even if that means paying for it.

Once you reach that point, you are back to the original question at the start of this chapter. Should we only stay in the Customs Union or should we embrace the Single Market? The answer lies in a single word – Services.

We hear a lot about "services" in the Brexit discussions, not least that they comprise around 80% of the British economy which is, let's face it, an awful lot – but what exactly are these services? The normal response jumps to industries like banking and insurance which are obviously very important but do not elicit a lot of sympathy from voters, especially those voters stuck in a wage trap in low-and middle-income jobs who have not seen their real wealth increase in a decade. They ask, not unfairly, why they should give a damn if the overpaid and pampered bankers and other financiers who trashed the economy in 2008 have to suffer a bit.

It is a point we shall revert to later, but before that it is also vital to understand that there's a lot more to services than just financial services. The broad term also encompasses travel and tourism (the world's largest employer), retail (i.e. shops and online retail), information technology, advertising and marketing, media and films, the vast range of often unloved "agencies" like estate and recruitment agencies and of course healthcare.

With most of the British population working in services,

the chances are high that you, reader, or your immediate family or your best friend earn your living within the broader service sector.

To put this in numbers, taking the figures from the Office for National Statistics in February 2018, the breakdown of the British workforce at that time was as follows:

Sector	Employees (thousand)	%
Agriculture and forestry	374	1%
Mining, energy, water supply	561	2%
Manufacturing and construction	5,273	16%
Services	26,023	81%
Total	32,231	

Source: Office for National Statistics, 2018.[29]

Hopefully that puts into context the issue we are talking about. Twenty-six million people in the UK work in services, four times as many as in the other sectors combined.

Of course, a lot of services are largely or purely domestic – health and education for example – but there is no question that exports of services are still vital to the national economy. Moreover, whereas we have a deficit in traded goods (we import more than we export), in services it is reversed. If you look at our exports to the EU plus Norway and Switzerland in

2016, we sold £157 billion of goods and £104 billion of services; while we imported £266 billion of goods and £80 billion of services. We therefore had a deficit of £109 billion in goods but a *surplus* of £25 billion in services.[30] In this vital sector, the mantra of "they need us more than we need them" is clearly nonsense.

An analysis of UK trade by the Centre for Economics and Business Research published in November 2016 estimated that of 1.9 million jobs directly linked to EU trade in the UK, and a further 1.35 million indirectly dependent on it (i.e. 3.25 million overall), a total of 2.1 million were in services, with 1.2 million of these being directly affected.[31] In other words, about 2/3rds of our trade-related employment is service-based.

Most importantly, financial services had exports of £96 billion in 2016 of which around £27 billion is sales to the EU.[32] The CEBR estimates that around 250,000 to 300,000 jobs depend on this.

As noted above, there may be little sympathy with employees in the financial services sector, but they pay a good deal of tax. If, on average, each of those employees pay £10,000 of tax per annum, the loss of 250,000 jobs would cost the UK exchequer £2.5 billion a year in lost tax revenue – that's one-third of the UK's annual contribution to the EU, just from one sector! That money pays for a good many nurses and teachers and if it disappears from our economy, so do they.

The sale of financial services to our EU and linked

European partners is a therefore a vital part of the British economy. And therein lies the problem – to date, no international trade deal covers financial services. Philip Hammond has made it clear that he would like our final trade deal to do so – the EU has made it clear they disagree. To date, the EU has won almost every point in the discussions – how likely are they to concede on this one; and if they do, what will they ask in return?

So much for trade, let us look at another vital part of the UK economy, inward investment i.e. investment by companies from outside the UK into the UK (also called foreign direct investment or "FDI"). The UK is very good at attracting FDI and it has lots of advantages that have nothing to do with the EU – the English language; the rule of law and a legal system whose basis is shared by many countries around the world; populations descended from immigrants linking us to many economies around the world; relatively liberal regulations; a tolerant attitude to outsiders; generally low business taxes; London, probably the world's most "global" city (at least before Brexit).

That is a powerful mix, but one factor not listed above is also immensely important – the ability of the UK to sell its products into the EU market of 512 million people. If you are a US or a Japanese company thinking about where to set up a factor or a warehouse in Europe, then that market is naturally more exciting than just the UK market of 66 million.

From 2005 to 2016, the UK secured an average of US$ 60.4 billion *more* than Germany each year in inward investments. In 2017, however, we were behind Germany by US$ 14.8 billion. (We were even behind Italy, the sick man of Europe, by US$ 2 billion!).[33]

The prospect of the UK leaving the EU single market has seen inward investment dry up – and very clearly companies like Nissan and Airbus are warning that continued investment in the UK depends on a good deal with the EU. At the time of writing, Panasonic has just announced that it will relocate its European headquarters from the UK to Amsterdam as a direct result of Brexit.

Again, for most people who don't work in a foreign-owned company, does any of this matter? It does and the earlier, rather boring section on trade is the reason why. As you may have noticed, the UK nearly always runs what economists call a "current account deficit". In plain English that means we buy more goods and services from abroad than we sell to other countries. In simple terms, our money is flowing out every year to pay for this.

There is nothing wrong with that in itself, but it does mean that we need to find other ways to get money into the UK to balance the books and we do that in two ways. One is inward investment and one is what we might call "short term capital movements". The latter basically means foreigners buying financial instruments issued by British entities, mainly in the form of debt: gilts issued by the Treasury and bonds issued by companies.

If inward investment falls, then the only way to keep funding ourselves is to get more money coming into those debt instruments. What makes investors want to buy debt? If it pays higher interest of course. What that means in practice is that if inward investment falls, and we need to get more foreigners to buy our debt, interest rates will rise...and suddenly all this boring economics comes home to roost. Higher interest rates mean higher mortgages and lower house prices; they also cause the stock market to fall (meaning smaller payouts on pensions and saving schemes that rely on shares).

For the millions of Britons with cash savings or who are trying to buy a house, that may seem like really good news, and for some it may indeed be so. However, the problem with falling house and share prices is that they are the main assets of people with money – and it is people with money (those wealth creators we talked about earlier) who spend money! There is a very clear correlation in the UK between house price increases and consumer spending.

If interest rates go up and spending falls, then the country enters recession – which means more unemployment, less tax revenue for the government and so another squeeze on public services. Bad news all round.

Let's sum up all of this economic stuff.

CHAPTER 5

Wealth creators generally do not like Brexit. They don't like it because:

1) We do a lot of trade with the EU and hundreds of thousands of jobs (maybe millions) depend on that trade

2) Any loss of our ability to export to the EU is not likely to be made up by trade treaties elsewhere

3) Services and especially financial services are vital to the UK economy and may well be outside any deal we sign (including the proposed Chequers deal)

4) Inward investment is also vital and if the eventual deal puts off investors, it will probably lead to both less jobs created by those investors and also to higher interest rates, with an increased chance of a recession

So if we ask: will Brexit support the UK's wealth creators, that second long-term pillar of Conservatism, the answer is that it will not. It will clobber them.

What about "Soft Brexit", the apparent compromise which so many moderate Conservative MPs have recently espoused, by arguing we should join the EEA or maybe recreate a new customs union from outside the EU but replicating many of the advantages of the current one?

There is no question that, economically speaking, it is better for Britain to be in a Customs Union with the EU than outside one even if that restricts our ability to sign trade deals with third parties. EEA status is a different approach, leaving us freer to trade (and outside EU fisheries and agriculture policy) but equally having to adopt some of the EU's "four freedoms" i.e. freedom of movement of goods, capital, services and labour. It would put us on the same plane as those other global powerhouses, Liechtenstein, Iceland and Norway, able to give our opinions on EU policy but not actually drive it. The EEA does take us outside the jurisdiction of the European Court of Justice, but would then put us under the jurisdiction of the EFTA court which is governed by the EFTA Surveillance Authority. Britain would be a big voice in EFTA but still – it's not complete independence, just a different division in which to play.

What all of these supposed "solutions" miss is two key elements of the debate:

a) As already discussed, if we are to keep exporting to the EU – and attract inward investment from companies which also want to export to the EU – we will have to adopt EU standards and regulations. In any of these Brexit scenarios we will not be shaping those standards. We will be a rule-taker not a rule-maker. However you dress it up, this is a position of impotence and will definitely, over time, put UK-based companies at a disadvantage.

b) Regardless of the economics, we would also be outside the power structures that govern our continent, a weaker and less powerful voice in the world. We will tackle that point later. For now, let's look at the second half of the economic story.

6. Will Brexit assist the government is pursuing a prudent spending policy ensuring job creation and maintaining a tax base which allows the government to provide the key services our citizens have a right to expect?

We now turn to the third pillar of Conservative policy over the ages: the combination of a balanced budget with taxes being set as low as prudently possible, while also bringing in enough money for the government to provide key services to citizens – and, at the same time, ensuring continued growth and job creation in the economy.

That may all seem like a mouthful, but it shows the way the Conservative Party has generally balanced its priorities. It has not, generally speaking, indulged in a "Tea Party-like" ideological crusade to lower taxes regardless of whether the reduced tax income means bankrupting the national budget; nor has it followed Labour in a tax-and-spend policy which reduces the incentives for companies to invest or citizens to save or to work harder and strive for more.

Instead, the Conservatives have followed a pragmatic set of economic policies, sometimes cutting back the growth in government spending as in the recent years of so-called "austerity", at other times loosening the purse strings.

Despite all of that, however, we find ourselves after eight years of Conservative-led government in a bit of a mess.

The Conservatives have been blamed for cutting back on spending, but like much else in today's political dialogues, this is to some degree a myth. In reality, between 2010 and 2018, government expenditure rose 21% (or, as the population also grew over that time period, by 15% per person). Spending on health rose 26% (or 20% per head of population). True, both education and policing have seen real falls (with the decline in education spending partly explained by converting student grants which appeared as spending, with students loans, which don't), but spending, far from being cut to the bone, has continued to rise.

If you adjust for inflation, the story is a bit different. Prices rose 24.5% from 2010 to 2015 and that means that the 21% increase in spending was actually a fall of 2.5% – and per head a greater fall of 7.3%. So spending has fallen, though perhaps not as drastically as the rhetoric would suggest.

Moreover, despite the Conservative rhetoric about getting the nation's borrowing under control, we have not only failed to dent the National Debt, it has actually risen dramatically from around £1 trillion in 2010

CHAPTER 6

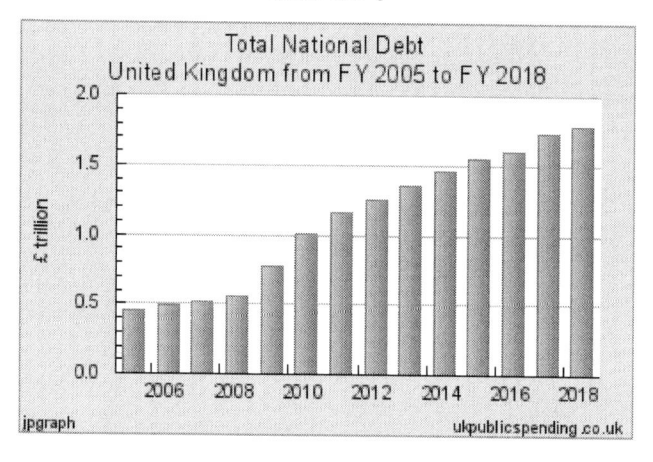

Total National Debt
United Kingdom from FY 2005 to FY 2018

(UK public spending, 2018)[34]

Despite that splurge of borrowing, it seems that our citizens feel, on average, that they are not getting better off and have felt that way for most of the past decade; and almost all of our public services are under unprecedented pressure.[35]

The latter is widely commented on but often met with a shrug. Like people who have lived in a house for too long, we cease noticing the stains on the carpet, the threadbare sofa, the dents in the walls and the damp stain on the ceiling. It takes a new buyer or tenant to see the run-down house for what it is.

British public services are a bit like that. We muddle along, we grumble quietly but we have lost sight of how serious the deterioration is and particularly of the fact that it has eroded almost everything the government does.

The armed forces are stretched to a point where they would be hard-pressed to defend our shores, let alone embark on a serious foreign war. Our hospitals are in perpetual crisis. Local councils have seen central government funding evaporate and are shutting down services. The police will often turn up to meet a crime victim merely for the purposes of informing them, politely, that they cannot help, usually due to a lack of resources. Schools are selling playing fields and asking parents to help buy books. Our roads and trains are overcrowded. There is almost no area of the state-funded economy that is in good shape.

The reality is that we are under enormous pressure as a country. Against a promise of ever-increasing living standards, prosperity has stalled and the government is struggling to fund its most basic spending requirements. To work out what is happening – and to see whether Brexit can help solve it – we need to look at a wider and deeper picture than most politicians would ever dare to address because the answers are not palatable. That is why you won't have read what follows in any mainstream press and won't have heard it uttered by any of the country's leading politicians.

The problems the UK faces are not unique – they are common to most of the countries in the West.

They revolve around:

An ageing population

Just 40 years ago, life expectancy in the West was

around 70 for males and 75 for females. Today, it is 79 for men and 83 for women – almost a decade more life. Clearly, a very large proportion of the population lives well beyond that average – meeting a centurion was exceptionally rare in the 1970s but is quite common today. This increase of 8-10 years in longevity has a double financial impact. Firstly, the state is paying far more in pensions and welfare than it was. Secondly, the pressure on the NHS has increased dramatically because the over- 80s require something like four times the amount of care needed by younger folk. That is why the NHS continually seems underfunded despite getting ever larger dollops of public cash.

Moreover, the retirement age has not moved up with life expectancy. In the 1970s, if a man retired at 65 and died at 70 the government paid for him for five years; today it is 14 years – nearly three times as long.

As a result, around 20% of all government spending goes on pensions.

As older people also require significantly more health care, the cost of the NHS is also impacted by an ageing population – the government will spend around £150 billion on healthcare in 2018 versus only £117 billion in 2010 with much more now promised for the future. Funding the NHS is always a priority for the British people in any survey and that is perfectly understandable – but it needs to be remembered that it is sucking resources out of the remainder of the economy.

A growing non-working student body

Pressure has mounted at the other end of the scale too – in 1950 just 3.4% of the population went to university – by 2017, participation in higher education hit 49%. Now, there is nothing wrong with people going to university or other higher education institutions, even if one might argue that university is not really appropriate for so many people and that technical training might be more useful to them. However, there is no denying that the same double-whammy applies at the bottom end of the age scale as at the top end – it costs money to maintain universities, and at the same time citizens in education are not paying taxes.

For a country increasing in prosperity every year – by more than the growth in population – the increased spending on education, health and pensions is just a normal part of becoming more civilised.

The problem is that we are barely doing that. In these circumstances, the massive expansion of higher education is more than the country has been able to afford.

A loss of competitiveness

Politicians do not ever really address it, but there has been a fundamental shift in the global economy over the past thirty years as China and India have locked into doing business with the rest of the world. It is too late to stop globalisation (though Donald Trump appears to be trying gamely to do just that, banging that stable door hard and repeatedly while the horse disappears off into the distance) but we must ultimately realise that it has had a profound impact on the UK. The modernisation of China and India, their ability to make goods far cheaper than we can but increasingly to the same standard, and the eruption of around one billion additional workers into the competitive global marketplace, has produced a field day for corporations and a very real problem for Western governments.

It wasn't supposed to be like this. The concept of globalisation was that emerging economies would make basic products like clothes while we made machines; they would advance into machines and engineered products while we advanced into IT and the knowledge economy; and would then get to the knowledge economy only once we had an unassailable lead in new areas like artificial intelligence, renewable power and nanotechnology.

That way, the West would stay ahead of the game, our economies would continue to boom and our workers would enjoy the ever-increasing bounty of capitalism – as would everyone else too.

Quite a lot has gone wrong with that.

a) The Asian economies have progressed far faster than was expected. Partly, as Trumpians would rightly argue, that was through a combination of protectionism and the theft of intellectual property, but in large part it was through sheer determination and reasonably sound economic management. As a result, China is a world leader, for example, in solar panels; and is catching up fast in areas like aviation and ballistics; India is the global hub for IT. Salaries in these countries are far lower than in Europe, so we are being out-competed even in cutting edge areas.

b) This has been reinforced by a work ethic, and a focus on educational excellence which has waned in the West...

c) ...and, at least in China, by governments which set long-term goals and stick to them, unimpeded by any risk of electoral disaster since they do not have competitive elections. We may not approve of that system, or want to live under it, but we equally need to acknowledge its efficiency in dragging a large population out of poverty.

d) Of equal importance is that the companies which have driven growth in the West are mostly multinationals like Google, Amazon, Facebook, Microsoft etc, and all have managed to shelter from taxes through their global structures. It is not their fault that they do so – all directors of such companies have a legal duty to their shareholders to maximise profits. It is the fault of governments in the West who have failed to get on top of this problem and levy sufficient taxes on such entities. As a result, vast amounts of profit are concentrated in the hands of these companies, being shared partly with their employees and suppliers but mostly between their shareholders. We capitalists may welcome such evidence of private enterprise, but when these companies are sitting on hundreds of billions of dollars of cash while the governments of our countries are effectively bankrupt, then there is a real problem. As government spending has soared, its revenues have fallen behind where they could be and, as government deficits have risen, services have been cut across the board – even while the share prices of new economy firms have surged.

The impacts of these trends are felt by real people right across the UK. In all Western economies, the share of business profits going to "capital" (shareholders) rather than "labour" (employees) has increased by about 20% points over the last 40 years. It does not matter whether their governments have pursued generally left-wing or right-wing agendas, the result has been the same – global forces have more than offset the relatively small impact of government policies.

To make matters worse, all of these trends have been greatly exaggerated over the past 10 years by the very low interest rates brought in to rescue the West's economies from the "financial crisis", a crisis itself created by the desire of individuals and companies to borrow far more than they could genuinely afford for far too long. While very low interest rates saved borrowers (and banks) from going under – and also helped governments to fund their own vast new borrowings – they also stoked up a whole new problem. When interest rates are very low, asset values such as house prices and share prices rise. On the other hand, people who put their savings into cash deposits make no money at all. Fairly obviously, it is the rich who own houses and shares and poorer people who put their money into bank and building society accounts. In consequence, the rich have got richer – the poor have seen their incomes and savings stagnate.

If ever there was a perfect lightning rod for channelling all the resulting discontent into a protest vote, it was the Brexit Referendum.

· *Feel left behind? – vote Leave; it can't get any worse!*

· *Think foreigners are taking your jobs? – vote Leave; we can stop them coming in*

· *Worried about a trade war with Europe? – well, they sell us more than we sell them so British jobs will be saved!*

· *Resent that smarmy Old Etonian who is running the country with his rich toff friends? – Vote Leave and give them a kick in the pants!*

To some, it all sounded so good, but after that vote, as the implications of leaving sink in, we need to ask ourselves whether leaving will actually solve any of those fundamental problems or whether, indeed, it might make them worse.

To keep the real goal in sight let's ask again: will Brexit

create jobs; will it give the government a bigger tax base and will it therefore allow the government to spend – prudently – greater amounts on vital services?

In order to ascertain that, we probably need to look at three of the main causes of the current problems and see whether Brexit can solve them:

1) Can Brexit reverse or slow the process of globalisation whereby Asian countries make goods cheaper than Europeans and so undercut us in many markets, making it hard to create jobs in the UK?

2) Will the UK, outside the EU, be better able to stand up to multinational companies which shelter their profits from governments around the world through complex corporate structures?

3) Will leaving the EU mean that cheap foreign workers are replaced across the UK by better-paid British ones? At least in Theresa May's mind and in the opinions of the harder-line Brexiteers, this is a very important part of the rationale for Brexit.

Let us examine these in turn:

1) Globalisation

Outside the EU, the UK will be negotiating on its own, not as part of the world's largest trading bloc.

In terms of challenging globalisation, the first problem we face is that the UK government does not want to! Indeed, one of the main promises of the Brextremists is that leaving the EU will free us up to trade *more* not less.

We are already a heavily trade-based economy. According to World Bank data, trade constitutes 58% of the UK's GDP versus 27% of the USA's, 37% of China's and 40% of India's.[36]

Like most of our European partners, our economy is highly trade-based and a move to put up barriers could be very damaging to us indeed.

Can these two issues be reconciled i.e. is it possible for us to become more global while at the same time sheltering ourselves from global competition? That would seem to imply that we would sign trade deals with countries like China, India and the USA in which they open their borders more widely to our exports at the same time as we partially *close* our borders to them.

That is pretty much the policy which Donald Trump is pursuing towards China, and it may be that he achieves at least some degree of success. However, the US economy is the largest in the world and, as we have just seen above, it is not very dependent on foreign trade – in fact, less so than any other major nation on earth! Starting from that situation, the US is in a far stronger position than the UK could ever be.

The sad reality is that the UK can only put pressure on other powerful nations to take the key steps towards rebalancing trade (opening up markets, improving working conditions, clamping down on intellectual property piracy, ending subsidies to emerging industries etc) as part of a powerful trading bloc like the EU. Alone, we are a far less compelling voice – the fifth or sixth largest economy in the world rather than the largest.

If we want the world's major economies to open up their markets to our companies, you can be absolutely sure that they will demand we further open our economy to their corporations (or, as with the case of India, to their workers). Our ability to resist such pressure will be pretty limited if we have just left the EU without having secured access to European markets or to the markets of most of the other 52 countries with whom our trade treaties will have fallen away at the same time.

2) Clamping down on tax-avoiding multinationals

Again, the Brexiteers' policies are not really looking to tackle this one. Instead, some of them promise that the UK will attract business by becoming a low-tax haven like (for example) Singapore. It is hard to see that there is much more upside here really, because the UK's corporate tax rate is already 19% and set to drop to 17% while Singapore's is....17%. So in all probability, any companies looking for a low tax base will already have been attracted to the UK.

If instead a post-Brexit government sought to raise the tax base by trying to capture more profits from the big multinationals, it is difficult to see how this could be achieved better outside the EU than within it. The EU has been a leader in anti-avoidance measures – witness its 2016 Anti Tax-Avoidance Directive which comes into effect in 2019; or the European Commission ordering Apple in 2016 to cough up €13bn in tax which it claimed had been underpaid in Ireland.

Indeed, nearly all serious attempts to prevent tax avoidance are being conducted by global bodies – for example, the OECD's BEPS (Base Erosion and Profit Shifting) project, which seeks to prevent companies artificially moving profits from higher-tax countries to lower-tax ones.

It is almost impossible for a single country to act alone on this because if you clamp down, another country can simply lure companies with rules which are more lax. There is little point, for example, in the UK cracking down if Ireland refuses to follow suit.

As with so many areas of the economy, working with our partners is far likelier to produce a positive result than going it alone.

3) Immigration

Lastly we come, of course, to the key issue which swung the Referendum – immigration; and especially the impact on UK jobs and wage levels of the large influx of workers from other EU countries over the past decade, let alone the supposedly vast numbers of benefit scroungers.

To see if Brexit will have the desired effect, we need to look at three linked but separate questions:

- Will Brexit put a stop to immigration from the EU?

- If it does, will it also mean that immigration numbers fall dramatically overall?

- And if those things happen, will wages and living standards for hard-working Britons rise?

At a very fundamental level, the answer to the *first* of those questions is yes, to a significant degree but of course not totally. While the UK will remain an attractive place for many EU workers due to the English language, a relaxed regulatory regime for both workers and entrepreneurs, existing communities of compatriots and low taxes, if all EU citizens will require work permits or even milder forms of registration to come to the UK, and face an uphill struggle to settle here permanently, it is highly likely that numbers will drop significantly. They will also be affected by a feeling that foreigners are less welcome; by the fall in the pound, which has made the UK a less attractive base for sending home foreign earnings; and by a potentially weaker economy which will mean fewer job opportunities.

Even since the Brexit vote and long before the date fixed for leaving, 29th March 2019, immigrant numbers from the EU have fallen – and as we have seen in the press, there has been a significant rise in the number of EU citizens leaving the UK – for example from the nursing profession. As the Guardian reported on 25th April 2018:

> *A total of 3,962 such staff from the European Economic Area (EEA) left the Nursing and Midwifery Council register between 2017 and 2018. The register tracks who is eligible to work in those areas of healthcare in the UK.*
>
> *The number of departures was 28% more than the 3,081 who left in 2016-17 and three times higher than the 1,311 who did so in 2013-14, the first year the NMC began keeping data on such departures.*
>
> *At the same time, the number of EU nurses and midwives coming to work in the UK has fallen to its lowest level. Just 805 of them joined the NMC register in 2017-18. That total is just 13% of the 6,382 who came over the year before*[37]

The NHS is just one example of British enterprises which have depended heavily on EU workers – they made up 10% of all doctors and nurses in the NHS up to 2016; but it is far from being the only one. Retail, restaurants, hotels and farms all depend very heavily on EU workers.

To see whether the reduction in the availability of EU workers will have the desired effect of making jobs more readily available for British workers at much higher pay, we can look at how a British company which employs a significant number of EU workers might react to their disappearance.

CHAPTER 6

The hope of the Brexiteers is that they will simply shrug and hire Brits instead, at salaries 20 or 30% higher. It is interesting that a Conservative, capitalist government would be swayed by such a simplistic assumption and indeed, shows how far from business the Tory Party has shifted. Anyone who knows about businesses will understand that – while a few companies will do just that, pay more for British workers – the vast majority will look for other options first. Businesses need to make a profit; for many businesses, labour is their largest cost, so they are not just going to sit back and see their profits reduced materially (or maybe even eliminated) rather than trying to mitigate the impact.

What might they do? There are three routes they may take to avoid paying more for a domestic workforce which has shown little inclination to get involved in many areas of the economy (eg fruit picking or waitering) and may demand uneconomic levels of pay in order to be lured into jobs in those sectors:

1) Some businesses will look to hire workers from elsewhere in the world. For more skilled jobs, even the "points-based system" much beloved of the Brexiteers allows in workers with skills from elsewhere. Indeed, since the Brexit vote, while net immigration from the EU has fallen, from outside the EU, primarily from Asia, it has increased. For less skilled jobs, there are always the illegals – whose numbers cannot (for obvious reasons) be quantified, but are believed to number between 0.5 million and

1.5 million, depending on what you read. They are clearly not from the EU as EU workers are, by definition, legal. Where are they coming in from? Presumably, mostly from North Africa and the Middle East, though again the lack of data makes it hard to know exactly.

2) Some will seek to increase efficiency, which is great for productivity and may indeed raise salaries but will not create new jobs; indeed, may well lead to fewer jobs for existing workers as processes are re-engineered to require fewer employees.

3) Some will move their operations (or the bulk of their operations) abroad, meaning a loss of jobs and taxes over here

4) Some, where possible, will seek to increase automation, again probably at the cost of jobs.

For some voters – and indeed for some civil servants and government officials – this may seem like a good outcome all round. Fewer immigrants; higher productivity; higher salaries for UK workers.

However, another group of companies will not be able to do any of the above – they will simply have to pay more for British workers; and if they can afford that, it's a good thing. In quite a few cases of course, they won't be able to – they will just go bust. A wave of restaurant closures in the South East is a case in point. The restaurant sector has been triply hit by the Brexit vote – higher food prices, an exodus of highly-paid workers who were their best customers and fewer low-cost employees from the EU.

Therein lies the downside. When a British employer who cannot afford the higher salaries goes under, it is not only the EU workers who have lost their jobs but the British ones in the same company. Moreover, with the loss of taxes from both the EU and the UK workers, and the need to pay benefits to the British ones (and in all probability, to many of the EU workers too if they remain in Britain), the government will have less money for schools, houses and the NHS. So in these cases, we all lose out.

In reality, we will see a mix of all these outcomes – some companies paying higher wages and improving productivity; some doing that but at the expense of British jobs; some hiring non-EU workers both legal and illegal; some replacing people with machines and some just going bust.

British workers, especially those in low-paid sectors or those in sectors where employees from the EU were serious competition will do better; equally, some British workers will lose their jobs. There may be some net benefit in terms of domestic wages, but it is likely to be small overall and will hardly offset all the other disadvantages of Brexit.

Moreover, immigration from elsewhere is likely to rise, as companies seek to replace departing EU workers. Whether Brexit will significantly reduce immigration overall is highly questionable. According to government statistics, the first quarter of 2018 saw migration of 322,000 people in to the UK, up from 302,000 in the first quarter of 2017. A fall of around 30% in migration from the EU – down to 87,000 was outweighed by a rise in non-EU migration of around 30% to 235,000 (a record for the last decade).[38]

Interestingly, both Sajid Javid and Liam Fox have said this summer that the "tens of thousands" immigration target will soon be reviewed, with the underlying hint being that it will be abandoned. Reality has come home to roost.

Before we move off immigration back to the main lines of discussion, it is worth understanding why the issue became so central to the 2016 Referendum and why, indeed, it has such an emotional pull for many voters. As noted above, the single term "Immigration" is used to cover a wide range of people-movements which are all rather different. It includes:

1) Migrations of workers within the EU

2) Immigration from outside the EU

3) Applications from asylum seekers and refugees, quite a few of which may be rejected

4) Illegal immigration – which may be people coming under false pretences, people overstaying visas, rejected asylum seekers and refugees refusing to leave or, at the extreme, people simply sneaking

CHAPTER 6

into the country, whether by boat or on lorries aboard the Eurostar

For the many citizens concerned about immigration, the concerns fall into an array of different buckets:

1) "Immigrants may take my job or undercut my pay by offering to work for less"

2) "Immigrants are clogging up the housing system, schools and increasing NHS waiting times"

3) "Within immigrant populations may be criminals or even terrorists"

4) Added to this is a cultural, religious and, for some, a racial dimension – a significant number of people are concerned about the dilution of the UK's Judaeo-Christian traditions, its liberal social attitudes, its pro-Western political orientations and in some less savoury cases, if we are honest, the colour of the skin of its inhabitants.

The Brexit campaign cleverly elided all of these fears together as epitomised by Leave.EU's infamous "Syrian migrants" poster.

The clear implication of the poster was that if we stay in the EU, we will be overrun by Asian refugees and asylum seekers – but actually the impact of leaving the EU is mainly to prevent Polish and Romanian workers coming to the UK. We are not obliged to take the asylum seekers who Merkel admitted to Germany and for the most part, we have not.

At the same time, Remainers should not sneer at the very real concerns expressed by voters about the impact of immigration. We have already dealt extensively with the belief that leaving the EU will help to preserve British jobs and maintain wage levels – and as we noted, while there is an element of truth in that, it is unlikely to be very effective.

What about the other immigration-related fears of Leave voters? These are well summed up in Douglas Murray's bestselling cri-de-cour *"The strange death of Europe"* which fears the loss of a "European lifestyle, culture and outlook" as a result of large-scale – and especially large-scale Muslim – immigration.

He notes the clash between modern tolerant European liberalism and the anti-gay, anti-feminist intolerance of extreme Islamists and asks whether, by being tolerant of intolerant people, we are in fact signalling our death knell.

While parts of the book may be uncomfortable and even offensive to those of us who have grown up in an era where we have been taught to accept and indeed revere cultural diversity, there are some home truths in the book which cannot be avoided and they arise from the difficulty of integrating literally millions people from a very different cultural background from that which we have enjoyed in Europe.

And yet the title of the book itself gives the lie to the Brexiteers – it is not called the strange death of Britain, but of Europe; it does not celebrate the peculiarities of our island race but rather the commonality of culture and outlook which we share with other Europeans.

What many Brexit-supporting voters were expressing was a concern that the UK was changing faster than they felt comfortable with, and that the people who are changing it bring with them a new set of attitudes which might not gel with British viewpoints.

They have a point but, as with so many other concerns which Brexit was supposed to address, it makes the problem worse, not better.

There may come a point where a higher birth rate, better training and increased automation mean that we no longer need to import workers to fill our booming industries – but it is some way away. In the meantime, the laws of economics say that unless we accept immigration at some level, we will run out of nurses and doctors, chefs and waiters, fruit-pickers and shelf-stackers. At present, they come mostly from East Europe. If the rules make it harder for these migrants, then new arrivals will inevitably come from North Africa and the Near East since they are the closest points to us. It is already happening – as EU immigration to the UK falls, so migration from elsewhere rises.

For those voters concerned about the line of asylum-seekers in the Syrian immigrant poster, the reality is that Brexit brings them nearer. You may not agree with the fear, or the attitudes which underlie it – but that doesn't mean it's not out there, influencing how many British voters behave.

Does that all mean that we should simply ignore immigration, sweeping it under the carpet as so many governments have done for the last 40 years? Emphatically, no – but the emphasis needs to combine education about the benefits which immigrants can bring to a society with a commitment to tackling the real unfairness and abuses of the system which have been allowed to fester unchecked. We need to step up genuine efforts to send home illegal immigrants and failed asylum seekers. Certainly, they should not be caught and them immediately released back into the community to disappear again as happens today. Within the EU, we should lead the charge to strengthen the overall EU external border, possibly *in extremis* looking with less prejudice at Australia's policy of processing asylum seekers outside the EU borders though in proper (and decently constructed) holding centres; and ensuring that genuine refugees are nurtured while illegal economic migrants are forced to leave.

If this sounds harsh, then it needs to be put into a

CHAPTER 6

historical perspective which is all too often lacking today. As somebody born into a Jewish family, I cannot help but think back to the 1930s. If European countries had admitted the Jews seeking to flee from Hitler but told them they had to spend a couple of years in a holding camp – or even maybe to work for free for their host country – I do not think many would have refused. *Genuine* refugees, fearful for their lives, generally will not object to paying their way or to being kept in austere conditions if it allows them sanctuary – and giving sanctuary to real refugees is a moral imperative for any civilised country.

Equally, for potential economic migrants who obey the rules, fill in the forms and wait, sometimes years, for an answer, there is no joy in seeing hundreds of thousands of illegal migrants given priority – priority housing, priority schooling, priority healthcare, just because they lied and cheated. Rewarding fraudsters is hardly "British fair play", it encourages ever more of them to "try it on" and it should be stopped.

On the flip side, as a modern Conservative Party, we must try to tackle the insular attitudes which make people fearful of outsiders. Social surveys show that citizens who fear immigrants are more plentiful in regions which have the fewest of them; more integrated areas show far greater tolerance. In other words, it is a fear of the unknown that prompts most of the nationalist and sometimes racist instincts in the British people; once we know some immigrants, for the most part we tend to like them!

Perhaps that's enough on immigration. Let's get back to the main narrative of this chapter, the debate about whether Brexit can boost the national finances so that we can tackle the pressing problems of today's world.

Any serious analysis makes clear that it will not work. It won't impede the process of job losses caused by globalisation nor will it improve the UK's ability to negotiate on those grounds with the main economic powers of the world. It will not make it any easier to tax multinationals. It may improve prospects for workers in industries where EU migrants were competing hard for jobs and pushing down salaries, but the impact is likely to be felt far, far less than the Brexiteers had hoped or promised.

What about the other points in this chapter – the cost of pensions/NHS and of a growing student body? As they are not directly linked to Brexit, it is impossible to make any very clear predictions, but a few things are clear:

1) In order to replace the exodus of EU doctors and nurses, we will either have to hire more from other foreign countries or pay more to train our own people. The government has already committed to doing the latter with Jeremy Hunt promising 5,000 extra nursing places, but with the ending of the

NHS bursary scheme, the number of applications to enrol in nursing training slumped:

Between 2010 and 2016, the number of applicants to nursing courses in the UK ranged between 61,800 and 67,400 a year, according to Ucas. In 2017 – the year that the funding model changed in England and NHS bursaries were scrapped in favour of standard tuition fee loans – this figure fell to 54,985. [39]

The Daily Telegraph notes that:

Health officials said they aimed to hire 5,500 nurses from India and the Philippines following an increase in the number of UK graduates abandoning the profession, and a sharp drop in the number of nurses coming to work in Britain from the EU. [40]

Nursing provides a salutary lesson for the rest of the economy. If significant numbers of young EU workers return to their countries of origin and even a few UK pensioners decide to come back from the EU, that will add, not reduce, the financial burden on the NHS

2) The same story applies to education. If you listen to some Brexiteers, international students, including those from the EU are a serious burden to the British economy. However a recent study by economics and politics consultancy London Economics concluded that the average benefit to the UK economy associated with each EU domiciled student was £87,000. Its report concludes:

Aggregating across the entire 2015/2016 cohort of first-year students, the total economic benefit of international students to the UK economy was estimated to be £22.6bn over the entire duration of their studies, of which £5.1bn is generated by EU students.[41]

This contrasts with costs to the UK of the EU students of £1.1 billion i.e. a net benefit of £4 billion or roughly £60 for every man, woman and child in the UK. Other studies, for example by Oxford Economics, come to similar conclusions.[42]

It must be clear that any policy which discourages EU students from coming to the UK will hurt the British economy and British taxpayers.

In addition to that, UK higher education is estimated to receive at least an average of £500 million per annum in research and development funding from the EU, which will also dry up after Brexit – or have to be replaced by British taxpayers.

The loss of these income streams will not reduce the burden of paying for education in the UK – they will raise it still higher.

In sum, therefore, Brexit makes the government's ability to balance its own books harder; it is likely to extend austerity rather than bringing it to a halt. Against that third key test of Conservatism, it is an abject failure.

At least if Brexit helped us hold our country together,

that might make the pain worth the gain. Will it do that? Let's examine that issue next.

7. Will Brexit help to preserve the United Kingdom?

The Conservative Party has always had within its ranks some degree of division between "Great Britain" and "Little England" i.e. between those who see a better future as part of a larger and more powerful body and those supporters, almost all in England, who would prefer the UK to split into its constituent parts.

However, within that split, there has always been an overwhelming majority for the United Kingdom option i.e. to support the Union of England, Scotland, Wales and Ireland (since 1922, Northern Ireland). So intense was our support for this that in 1909 the party combined with a split-off from the Liberal party called the Liberal Unionists to create a new party, the Conservative and Unionist Party; and came close to backing armed mutiny in 1914 over the prospect of recreating an Irish parliament.

Similarly in both the 1974 and 2014 referenda on Scottish independence, the Conservatives campaigned strongly for Scotland to remain in the Union – the latter time under the slogan "Better Together".

The party has supported the Union since 1707 – over 300 years – and done so despite the subsidies paid out by England to the other nations in the Union, despite the Irish troubles, despite non-Conservatives generally winning the majority of the seats in all three other nations, despite votes from Scotland and Wales often tipping the scales in the Commons against a Tory-dominated England.

Why? Because Conservatives know that the skills and resources of our four nations make us stronger as a combined entity than when we are disunited (and indeed, potentially enemies of each other). There has never been a great English empire, let alone a Scottish, a Welsh or an Irish one, only a British one, the product of a powerful Union pooling its resources.

So if a policy threatens the Union quite severely, it is surely something to be considered very carefully under the heading "is it worth it?" After working so hard to keep our great nation together, are we prepared to just throw it away (or even to make the risk of disintegration materially higher)?

And Brexit does just that – it increases the likelihood that Scotland will demand additional devolved powers and, at some point, may even look to leave the UK and rejoin the EU as an independent nation. Recent polling suggests that supporters of an independence vote would again be ahead in Scotland after Brexit.

It also vastly adds to the problems of the situation in Northern Ireland, where the two communities, Unionist and Nationalist have found a slightly sullen acquiescence in an open border to be a lot less painful than open warfare.

Let us look at each situation in turn.

Scotland is in a difficult position post the Brexit vote. It voted overwhelmingly to Remain and secures a lot of subsidies from the EU – around €900 million between 2014 and 2020 from the Regional Development Fund and Social Funds alone.[43]

However, the nationalists were defeated in the independence Referendum and the SNP further lost ground at the last election; and for sure, with both oil and financial services subdued, the economic prospects for independence look grim. So, Scotland has little option but to stay with the UK for now, which is good news.

Less good is that if Britain exits the EU, a whole raft of powers exercised by the EU will come home – and the SNP is demanding that Scotland (and Ireland and Wales) secure a vast swathe of these, rather than having them go to Westminster.

This puts the government in a tricky position – if they devolve a further set of responsibilities to the Scottish Parliament, they further weaken the integrity of the UK; if they do not, they may stoke nationalist sentiment and push up the SNP vote – so further weakening the integrity of the UK.

The total mess of Westminster politics and especially the perception that all of the UK is now held captive by an internal fight in the Conservative Party also damages the credibility of the concept of Union. The SNP may not be a particularly competent administration, but they are not engaged in a decades-long civil war which has dragged the country down with them. The mess we are making of Brexit is as good an argument as Nicola Sturgeon could want for why Scotland would be better off freed from the shackles of Westminster.

Currently, another Scottish independence vote seems a distant prospect. Unfortunately, if Brexit crashes the economy, sentiment could turn again, with the reaction boosting the populist nationalism of the SNP.

Of more immediate risk is the situation in Northern Ireland. It is easy to forget that over 3,600 people died – and many more were maimed and injured – during the "Troubles", the period of 30 years of near civil war between the Nationalist/Catholic-based terrorists of the IRA and its spin-off bodies and the British government and Unionist paramilitary groups. The situation has been much calmer since the Good Friday Agreement was signed in 1998, but it remains fundamentally unstable. The problem is very simple. The Unionist population (i.e. supporters of remaining part of the UK) is a minority on the island of Ireland but a majority in the six provinces of Northern Ireland. The Nationalists (supporters of a United Ireland outside the UK) remain a minority in Northern Ireland but are demographically heading for a majority, largely due to a higher birth-rate than the mostly Protestant

Unionists. If they were to become a majority, a new crisis might break out, with a so-called "border poll" which offered voters a choice of putting all of Northern Ireland into the Republic; or maybe of redrawing the border to shrink Northern Ireland still further.

The European Single Market has, however, taken a good deal of the steam out of the problem, combined with the policy of an open border. Catholics in Northern Ireland can cross freely in and out of the Republic and essentially feel that they are all part of a single community. Protestants can also see the economic benefits of co-operation while still being able to remain part of the UK. It is an arrangement which suits everyone and if it is a fudge, then it's a fudge that works and saves lives. If the border were to be enforced, one or other sides of this argument may well feel aggrieved and violence could begin again. Several Brexiteers have condemned the making of this point as a surrender to the threat of violence but that is really quite disingenuous. If the IRA or a similar splinter group started up the "armed struggle" again, we would stand up to them firmly, imprison them and doubtless if there were armed attacks, the police and army would end up shooting quite a few of them. We might, conceivably, "win" a new war though most likely it would just drag on interminably, ruining lives and families and once more impoverishing Northern Ireland. People in the remainder of the UK may find the motivations for sectarian violence ludicrous and primitive in a modern world – as indeed they are – but it does not mean that we can simply ignore the risk and the consequences of stirring the pot again.

There is a cost element too. If one of the reasons for leaving the EU is to save the £8-9 billion annual contributions to EU coffers, it is worth noting that the costs of the Troubles, in terms of extra policing and a military presence, lost economic activity and conflict-avoidance measures were estimated a decade ago at up to £1.5 billion per annum.[44] There is a very real peace dividend which even a heartless government, unconcerned about the human cost of re-igniting conflict, would need to consider in the balance of pros and cons underlying Brexit.

As of now, Northern Ireland poses a pretty-much insoluble problem for the government. The 310-mile frontier between Northern Ireland and the Republic of Ireland is the UK's only land border with the EU and it has multiple crossing places. The government has pledged to keep an this an open border, but at the same time insists that the UK will leave the Customs Union while Ireland remains within it.

One solution which has been considered is that Northern Ireland could stay in the Customs Union while the rest of the UK leaves it. However, that is tantamount to creating, in economic terms, a united Ireland. This is hardly what the Conservative and Unionist Party should be about – forcing British citizens towards a foreign government. Moreover, May's administration relies on the goodwill of the Democratic Unionists who are adamantly opposed to any steps which might further Irish unity.

Another possible solution, which the British government has already agreed to, is that Northern Ireland will remain in "regulatory alignment" with the South. What that means is anybody's guess. If it remains in full regulatory alignment on everything, it has effectively stayed in the Single Market and would then rapidly find itself out of alignment with the rest of the UK – just what the Democratic Unionists want to avoid. Alternatively, maybe the whole of the UK would adopt regulatory alignment with the EU which is an entirely sensible position but of course the opposite course to that upon which the government is embarked. Moreover, Michel Barnier, the EU's chief negotiator has made it clear that the UK will not be allowed Single Market membership "by the back door".

Nor is there any real answer as to how to have a closed border for trade purposes but an open one for all others. The UK government tried arguing that this can be done by technology, but no other country took this seriously – even very friendly borders like those between Canada and the USA or Norway and Sweden still have physical checks. Moreover, the government (as all too often) only sees matters from its own perspective. It is basically saying to the EU "there's no problem about goods coming into Northern Ireland from the Republic; we're relaxed about it, it can be solved by technology". They forget that goods go the other way i.e. from North to South (perhaps for example, chlorinated chickens or hormone-fed beef imported from the US) and that the EU also has a right to be comfortable with the regulatory and inspection regime and would reject any solution which does not give it that comfort.

So the latest proposal is that we effectively remain in a single market for goods but not for services and that we collect EU tariffs at the UK border on the EU's behalf. At the time of writing it seems unlikely that Brussels accept this proposal.

It appears that the only answer – which is now in the draft documents on the "deal" as a backstop, is that from an economic point of view, Northern Ireland will be ceded to the Republic, with a customs barrier being created across the Irish Sea. Quite how any Conservative government could begin a process of forcing a loyal province out of the UK in the interests of "national sovereignty" and possibly reigniting a deadly conflict as the price for this, is very difficult for many Conservatives to understand. It is as un-Conservative a policy as it is possible to create – a betrayal of our national unity for the sake of Little Englander ideology.

To answer the fourth point then, Brexit does not bring the country together, it drives us apart, alienating Scots from the English and reinforcing differences within Northern Ireland which were beginning to heal.

So far, Brexit isn't scoring too well – nought out of four

CHAPTER 7

in terms of being compatible with core Conservative principles.

So let's look at the final one of the five key Conservative philosophies, one on which surely all Tories are united – the need for law to prevail over anarchy.

8. Does Brexit help the Rule of Law; and the maintenance of law and order?

Just to be clear, these are two very different concepts, however similar they may sound. The first, the "rule of law" describes a system whereby judges are independent and impartial and everyone is treated equally under the law. It is an age-old concept which goes back to the Magna Carta and underpins every functioning democracy – indeed, the problem with many recently-crafted "democracies" is that although they hold elections, the rule of law is largely absent, so allowing businessmen and politicians to buy immunity from the law.

Law and order is something different if overlapping, representing the ability of the state to protect its citizens from crime via an efficient police force, a functional legal system and a punishment/reform programme for criminals.

For the rule of law to function, politicians and businesspeople cannot be immune from due process and judges need to be able to make independent judgements. The way Brexit is being enacted threatens both of these vital pillars of the British constitution.

We have seen politicians tell factual lies with complete

impunity and even those MPs who oppose them accepting it with a shrug, as though telling the British people that trust is an optional extra in their profession. We have seen those same Brextremist politicians and their media backers describing judges who rule against them as "enemies of the people", as though we live in a fascist dictatorship where threats can be made against anybody not under the control of the prevailing ideology. We have seen electoral rules systematically and criminally circumvented. We have seen Parliament snubbed and a minority government wriggling every which way it can to avoid proper scrutiny of the most momentous decisions the country has faced in a lifetime.

It is a slippery slope away from the traditions of decency, honesty and fair play on which this country was built and to which the vast majority of our people want it to adhere.

Even for those (the vast majority) who are less concerned about constitutional niceties, there are real dangers which arise from Brexit in the more day-to-day sphere of catching criminals. Crime today is not just a national phenomenon. Many of the most serious crimes – drug-smuggling, people trafficking, the illegal arms trade, financial fraud – are all carried out internationally, often by global gangs and cartels. Terrorism too knows no borders, with even our home-grown terrorists being trained in camps in the Middle East or radicalised over the internet.

CHAPTER 8

One of the main elements of the Brexiteers' "Project Scare" was to suggest that by remaining in the EU, Britain would weaken its defences against Islamic terror, whether from Syrian refugees or by millions of Turks pouring across our borders.

It was such arrant nonsense that it needs to be tackled head-on.

Firstly, the UK had, has and will continue to have – inside or outside the EU – its own border controls. We are not part of the Schengen free movement area and anyone legally entering the UK will have their documents checked. Needless to say, illegal immigrants will not – but they would be coming in illegally even if we are outside the EU, so Brexit makes no difference to them.

Secondly, even if we were outside the EU, unless we imposed draconian visa restrictions on all visitors from the EU, terrorists would always be able to cross the border as tourists or businesspeople, carry out their foul misdeeds and then attempt to cross again – just as the attempted murderers of Sergei Skripal seem to have done. If we were to impose draconian visa checks on all visitors to the UK, it would not only cripple our massive tourism industry as well as more general commerce, but would surely lead to similar checks being imposed on Britons going abroad. It is not an option. So "terror tourism" could continue regardless of Brexit.

Thirdly, the only way to tackle serious cross-border

crime is through enhanced – not reduced – co-operation with our neighbours. Even Theresa May, who appears to be even more concerned about immigration than the most ardent Brexiteers, fought to keep the UK within the European Arrest Warrant ("EAW") system, so that we are able to extradite dangerous criminals to other EU countries with a relatively simple and low-cost procedure – and they are equally able to send our wanted criminals back to face British justice under the same system. It is estimated that 1,000 Britons wanted by our courts have been returned to the UK under this system and we have sent back 10,000 suspected criminals to other countries since 2004.

However, now, because of the government's refusal to continue to accept the jurisdiction of the European Court of Justice in any way, shape or form, the UK will have to leave the EAW system.

Even the *Daily Telegraph*, trumpet of the Brextremists, had to admit that even if we could negotiate a new extradition treaty with the EU, it would not apply to 18 member states which "have constitutions that bar the extradition of their own nationals to anyone outside of the EU".[45]

The logical impact of this move is thus that the UK becomes a far safer haven for criminals from EU states and may become a hub for fugitives from justice. Fairly obviously, that makes Britain a less safe place. So, Brexit is weakening the forces of law and order, not strengthening them.

CHAPTER 8

Oh dear! Nought out of five.

9. And what about Sovereignty?

Up to now, we have not touched on the Brexiteers' magic word, sovereignty, the word which underpins their slogan of "take back control" and which appears sufficient, from their perspective, to excuse any and every downside which Brexit may create.

We haven't because it is not actually a true Tory concept – it is much too amorphous. It sounds good; but trying to pin it down to anything meaningful is like trying to nail jelly to the ceiling.

What does "sovereignty" give us the power to do? Whose sovereignty is it? Who is included and who is excluded?

Today, our sovereign state is the United Kingdom of Great Britain and Northern Ireland. That means that the English, Welsh, Scots and Northern Irish have decided to pool the sovereignty of our different nations into a single political whole. It was not always thus. Between 1800 and 1922, the UK included Southern Ireland. Before 1707, Scotland wasn't part of it. Up to 1797, we claimed the French throne and indeed for long periods in our history we ruled large chunks of France – at times, more than the French king. (Or you could also argue conversely that Franco-Norman kings ruled England throughout the late Middle Ages).

In 1940, at the height of the German advance into France, as noted earlier, Winston Churchill offered the French an "indissoluble union" of our two countries to ensure that they could carry on fighting even if the continent fell. So, there is not really any one clear historical entity which has exercised sovereignty on our behalf – it keeps changing.

Then, within that entity, the second question we ask is – who is sovereign? Clearly, in terms of wording the Sovereign is sovereign i.e. the Queen is the ruler. However, over the years, royal power has been stripped back to almost nothing; just a few ceremonial roles and a weekly audience attended by the Prime Minister. We say, instead that Parliament is sovereign but again that is misleading. There are two Houses of Parliament, the Lords and the Commons and the power of the Lords is severely constrained. So do we live in a world where the real sovereignty lies in the House of Commons? You would like to think so perhaps, but actually the actions of MPs are almost entirely governed by their party whips who take instructions from party leaders, who are – these days, selected by party activists. Certainly, anyone looking at the current House of Commons where only the most extreme 60 Labour and 60 Tory MPs are in charge of the agenda of their two parties might conclude that a dictatorship of political activists is now sovereign. And then, of course, there is the "will of the people", expressed in various random referenda, called by party leaders who want to duck responsibility for key issues because keeping their

CHAPTER 9

parties together is more important than governing the country. These popular votes are deemed to be everlasting – until it is more convenient to overturn them with another referendum, just as the 1975 result was overturned in 2016.

So, it's all a bit complicated. Who really makes the decisions? Clearly, all of these groups – Queen, the Lords and the Commons, the parties, the activists and the voters all have varying degrees of power and the balance of that power is fluid – it changes over time.

Which brings us to the third and most important issue – what does sovereignty actually give us the power to do? As a sovereign nation we could, of course, declare war on America but we don't – because we would lose (and also of course because it would not be very nice – but this is a discussion of power, not morality). There is no point at all in having sovereignty if you are unable to use it.

The best example of this I have ever heard relates to Belgium between the wars. Germany, remember, had started the First World War by invading Belgium to get round the French defences. So after the war was won, the French decided to build an "impregnable" defensive wall, the Maginot Line, between it and Germany. Unfortunately, the geography was unchanged so the gap was still there to the north of the Maginot line, where the Franco-German border ended. The French proposed extending the Maginot Line along the Franco-Belgian border, to complete its own defences, but of course that left Belgium completely exposed to German attack and the Belgians did not like that one bit. To resolve that issue the French then proposed building it along the border between Belgium and Germany instead. "Oh no, you can't do that", said the Belgians, "it would be an infringement of our sovereignty". So the line never got extended, the Germans just went round it again and the Belgians – and of course the French too – were conquered. In defending their sovereignty, the Belgians lost their independence – a theoretical triumph which became a disaster in practice.

Today, having learnt their lessons from examples like that, many countries prefer to "pool" sovereignty. That means they share some of their rights with other countries in order to be stronger together.

This too was advocated by no less a Conservative than Winston Churchill:

In 1950, Churchill warned of "disadvantages and dangers of standing aloof" from Europe, stating that the [Conservative] opposition was "prepared to consider, and if convinced to accept, the abrogation of national sovereignty, provided that we are satisfied with the conditions and safeguards".[46]

Was Churchill wrong?

Before discussing the broad theoretical arguments, first let us look at how the idea of "better together" works on a more immediately human scale.

CHAPTER 9

Today, very few people choose to live alone. Whether it is kids living with parents, partners setting up home together, flatmates sharing, or elderly folk living with their children or in a residential or nursing home, most people, if they can, prefer to cohabit.

And, as we know, that is not always simple. Anyone involved in a battle for the TV remote, or an argument about the washing-up rota, or trying to stop old Mr Jones walking around the nursing home with his trousers falling off, or getting into massive rows about students tidying their rooms, or who gets to invite their friends round on which days……anyone in these situations knows that living with other people isn't easy.

Why do we do it then? It is not just for company and the avoidance of loneliness. Of course that is a factor but it can be overcome by having lots of friends, joining clubs and societies, popping round to the neighbours, taking up a course….even joining a political party!

The real reason people cohabit is because the downside is outweighed by the upside. Costs are shared; ideas pooled and problems jointly solved; we feel safer – somebody is there to look out for us.

It is the same for countries too. Why do the English, Scots, Welsh and Irish agree to be jointly ruled? Because we are stronger a single unit. We have disagreements but also mechanisms for working them out peacefully; we have a larger market to offer businesses; a bigger population to defend the homeland; a wider pool of talent on which to draw. Just as Angles and Jutes threw in their sovereignty with the Saxons to fend off the Vikings, so too home countries joined their sovereignty into a Greater whole – "Great" Britain and Northern Ireland". As a Conservative, that Union is a very precious thing.

But it doesn't stop there. Perhaps the greatest sacrifice of sovereignty is giving up the right to decide when to go to war, and with whom. Are Conservatives prepared to share that right with other countries? Resoundingly, yes. Not only do we do it, we embrace it, in the form of NATO membership, as the cornerstone of our defence strategy. Being in NATO means that if Russia were to invade Estonia, Britain would be at war – and against a nuclear-armed enemy. Are Tory MPs rushing to denounce that astonishingly important surrender of our independence of action? I have yet to hear it.

The EU of course, is slightly different. It makes laws and, under EU rules, they take precedence over domestic laws and that's what gets the Brexiteers' goat. How scary is that? What are we gaining and what are we losing? Does Brexit solve the problem?

The obvious consideration is whether what we gain outweighs what we lose and that has been the basis of how the Conservative Party has looked at the pooling of sovereignty up to 2016. The Brextremists' arguments are phrased in a way that suggests we gain nothing at all, but that is far from the case. Just as other countries have a say in laws that now govern the UK, we also get a say in laws that govern all 27 other members. Indeed, as one of the EU's most influential members we have a degree of power over other European countries of which Richard I or Henry V could only dream. Yes, we sometimes get outvoted but not very often – we are on the winning side more than nine times out of ten. That is real power – an extension of our sovereignty over others, rather than a diminution of it. Of course, if we are outside the EU, we are the losers in 10 out of 10 such decisions – they are made without us and without the interests of British business or citizens being raised and defended in the discussions.

And the alternative if we leave? Whether the UK likes it or not, we live in a multilateral world. If we leave the EU without a deal our trade will be governed by the World Trade Organisation over which we have far less influence than the EU. And, as discussed extensively, if we want to sell to the EU, by far our largest market, our goods will have to meet EU regulations and standards, over which we will have no say.

We would not have taken back control, we would have given it away.

Of course, one key plank in the Brextremist argument is that the EU is "undemocratic".

That claim does not stand up to even brief scrutiny. The EU is run by a combination of the European Parliament which is directly elected by voters from across the member states and the Heads of Government, including our own, who are also elected by their different national electorates. Nothing undemocratic there. It's true that turnouts in European elections are low – but they are in British council elections, too, and nobody is claiming that local councils aren't legitimate. It is also true that the European Commission – its Civil Service – proposes laws but that's not so different from British civil servants drafting legislation for Parliament to consider. As here, unless the Parliament and the governments approve laws, they don't happen. True, the Commission takes a rather bigger role than our Civil Service but it has to because somebody in a network of 28 countries has to take the lead – you can't criticise the EU for being cumbersome on the one hand and then also criticise it for having some processes to streamline decisions on the other.

The only real basis for the claim that the EU is undemocratic is the argument advanced way back in that vote NO pamphlet in 1975 that sometimes decisions will be taken in which the UK is outvoted; that is true, but it is true for everyone else too. There are also times when we will be outvoting Germany or France or Spain or Italy. Just like having to share the remote, if we generally find it preferable to be a leading player in a powerful community, we're prepared to accept that others will win the argument from time to time.

So, to sum up, sovereignty is a weak conceptual idea with far less to recommend it than real, deliverable power. Most countries in the world now share sovereignty to a greater or lesser degree and they do so to gain benefits, economic, political or military, which they cannot get by standing alone. Leaving the EU would not hand us our sovereignty back in an interconnected world; we would become more dependent on others' goodwill than ever before in our history.

Moreover, the pooling of sovereignty for greater collective strength is a concept very familiar to and accepted by successive Conservative governments, whether in NATO, the EU, the UN, the WTO or any other body which can instruct governments to do things they may not wish to. We do so for reasons of national self-interest not because we are deliberately trying to reduce our independence and we have gained as a nation from doing so.

10. Conclusions – Is Brexit Conservative?

If we return to the start of this study and look at the five key Conservative beliefs:

1) Keeping the country secure from foreign enemies

2) Supporting the wealth creators in the country, ranging originally from landowners when farming was the country's main economic activity, through to industry and now to the technology and service sectors – in the firm belief that if wealth creators can succeed and create jobs, there will be economic security for everyone in society

3) Maintaining a sensible and balanced fiscal policy, combined where possible with the lowest reasonable taxes

4) Belief in preserving the Unions with Scotland and (now Northern) Ireland

5) Maintenance of the rule of law; and of law and order internally

it is clear that Brexit is deeply damaging to all of them

1) It both distances the UK from our foreign allies in Europe and also reduces national prosperity,

so making it more difficult to afford rearmament in the face of the growing Russian threat and the long-term rise of the Asian giants

2) It hits almost every group of wealth creators in the UK and is opposed by virtually all of them;

3) By making the country poorer, it also makes it difficult for the government to achieve balanced budgets – indeed, increased spending to support the likely rise in unemployment which Brexit will cause is going to unbalance the country's finances still further

4) It makes a split with both Scotland and Northern Ireland more likely; and may cause sectarian problems to flare up again in the latter

5) It will make it harder to contain international crime; and the ideological fervour of the Brextremists, with their attacks on judiciary and Lords, calls into question the long-term rule of law, free from political coercion

It is clear that, with the possible exception of reducing legal immigration, at least from the EU, Brexit solves none of the issues our country faces and indeed, makes most of them worse.

If then Brexit will weaken our international influence, make the country poorer, render our armed forces less effective, threaten the unity of our Kingdom and potentially make policing our streets harder, it looks far closer to high treason than patriotism. How can it ever have become Conservative policy? Why should any good Conservative support it? What is driving the Brexiteers? Why have they succumbed to a partisan fervour as blinkered as Communism or Fascism, willing to inflict any hardship on the country in their zeal for ideological purity?

Clearly they believe they are in a desperate fight to save the UK from a Brussels superstate which, if it were a real possibility, might indeed be quite scary. Fortunately, it is not real. For all their lip-service to an ever more united Europe, countries like France and Germany have no desire to dissolve themselves – and other, newer members like Austria, Hungary and Poland are in thrall to some quite aggressive nationalism which is miles away from the European Federalism of the isolationists' nightmares. Yes, Europe will, by fits and starts, gradually move closer together, but it will remain a supranational alliance, not a single country – at least not for the next 100 years or more.

Moreover, in continually highlighting the drawbacks of Europe – the difficulty of reaching a consensus among 28 countries, the premature rush into the Euro, the corruption in some member states, the unwieldly arrangements for the European Parliament etc – we tend to lose sight of all the positives which the EU brings, regardless of the weakness of its institutions or some of its recent policy mishaps.

Let's look at those for just a minute.

The first, of course, is peace. When, during the Referendum, David Cameron raised this, he was immediately mocked by Boris Johnson as threatening World War Three. As usual with Boris, the mocking got him headlines, but was essentially shallow and unthinking. Of course, Britain leaving the EU does not lead immediately (or even relatively soon) to a new war on the Continent of Europe. But it does threaten the unity of the West, it will take us out of the decision-making on key issues like maintaining sanctions against Russia or imposing them on states like Iran and North Korea. It also weakens our voice in encouraging our neighbours to meet their NATO spending commitments and it does make it more likely that the EU may gradually drift away from the USA.

All of those points assume of course that the global geopolitical architecture will remain largely static i.e. that a united West will be in a stand-off with Russia and eventually China, backed up by US military might and especially its nuclear arsenal. Well maybe – at least for now. But history doesn't actually work that way. Countries' interests change and former allies may eventually transform themselves into competitors and then ultimately enemies. Who would have thought in 1945 that Germany would soon be a firm ally in standing up to Russia? Who would have thought in 1898 when we were almost at war with France and fearful of a Russian descent on British India that we would soon be allied to those two countries against a Germany united under a Prussian state which British influence had helped to expand as a bulwark against France in the aftermath of Napoleon? The world is unpredictable.

What the EU has done, in this uncertain world, is to bind together 512 million people who have spent most of the last 1,000 years at war with each other. War between member states is essentially unthinkable.

And for those Tories, probably in many cases Brexiteers, with little interest in geopolitics or the balance of power, let us not forget that war, and preparing for war, is vastly expensive. If a major conflict were imminent, our contributions to the EU budget would appear as inconsequential as a drop of rain against the tens, indeed hundreds of billions we would need to allocate to defend ourselves against a Europe aligned against us or controlled by an enemy.

While that seems impossible today, it is foolhardy to ignore the fact that countries are either growing together or growing apart. The EU ensures the former, and the peace dividend it has produced is what has allowed Britons to enjoy the living standards which prevail today.

Peace itself brings prosperity, but so – rather more mundanely – do free trade and regulatory alignment. Being in the EU gives companies based in the UK access to that market of 512 million, allows our professionals to practise across the Community, allows our companies and public services like the NHS to access the labour market of the entire EU – all of which makes the country richer, increases the government's tax revenue and so allows it to spend more on the NHS and schools and the police than it could do otherwise.

Remainers were hopeless at making this case, but there is a lot further to go in developing the Single Market and most of the next steps, in liberalising sectors where the UK is strong like IT, telecoms and financial services, would benefit our economy enormously.

So, apart from peace, prosperity and the aqueducts, what have the Europeans ever done for us? There is free movement of course. Leavers have managed to paint that in an awful light – a means for nasty East Europeans to come over and steal our jobs. We have dealt with the likely consequences of leaving the EU and ending free movement in that regard earlier in this book but we have not yet looked at the positives of free movement:

- The right of British pensioners to retire in any EU country they choose and to get benefits and healthcare there

- The right of British students to study in any EU country, often assisted by the EU's Erasmus programme

- The right of British workers to work anywhere within the EU

- The right to travel within an open community,

to use those shorter immigration lines, to have access to the EU's healthcare when abroad, to get free roaming or our mobiles

For very many UK citizens, free movement has been good, not bad!

Finally, there is strength. As a leading power in the world's richest integrated economic bloc, containing two nuclear-armed powers, the UK is strong. We can punch above our weight in the world – which, even if we pretend otherwise, is what most Conservatives want to see us doing. While Brexiteers like to twitter on about the UK being the world's fifth largest economy, it is our lynchpin role between the USA, Europe and the Commonwealth, binding them together in a way that no other country can hope to do, which gives us our pivotal position in the world. Outside the EU, we are of less use to the USA in its dealings with Europe and less use to the EU in its discussions with America. Even the leading Commonwealth countries, so opposed to the UK joining the EEC in 1973 have all urged us to stay in the EU now. Certainly, their voices will be weaker within the EU bloc without the UK to fight their corner.

So, EU membership gives us strength, peace, prosperity and freedom. It is not a bad combination and it does so without forcing the UK to join the bits of the EU we don't like – the Schengen free movement area and the Euro. Within the EU we kept our border control and we kept the pound. (If we leave and, based on the votes of a younger generation, decide to rejoin later, it is not likely that these opt-outs will still be on the table for us).

Yes, there are downsides but the upsides massively outweigh them. But even if you do not agree with that, even if you would rather be outside, you are barking up the wrong tree. As the basis of everything they believe, Tory Brextremists have made one key assumption which is wrong.

At its heart, the Tory split over Europe is based on just one fundamental question – is Europe a **fact** or an **option**?

If that sounds a bit banal, that's because the issue is really very simple indeed.

If you see Britain's place in Europe as genuinely an option, it is quite easy to press a switch called "OUT". Once that switch has been pressed, your worldview then says that you are, at that instant, completely free. Britain is free to choose where to trade, with whom to ally, who to allow into the country; we are subject only to our own courts and our own laws.

If, however, you see Europe not as an option but as a fact, inescapable and unavoidable, then the story changes dramatically. It becomes very clear that turning our backs on the Channel and burying our heads in the Dover sands does not make Europe go away. It is still there, glistening in the dusk, 26 miles away. It is still our largest trading partner. To sell into it, we will still need to meet its regulations and standards. To work within it, we will still need to have our citizens' qualifications accepted. If we have labour shortages, it is the simplest and overwhelmingly the safest source of new migrants. Above all, it is from where all threats to our fundamental security have always originated, which is why our foreign policy has never veered far from ensuring that we hold the balance of power in what is our own continent.

The Brexiteers, of course, see Europe as an option. Remainers see it as a fact. Remainers are right.

And that is why, as the months since the Referendum have unfolded, the Leave promises have crumbled away and the Remain warnings have increasingly been revealed as far-sighted.

The EU is far from perfect. It rushed the expansion to the East (at the behest of British Conservatives, it might be added) bringing in new countries before either their economies had converged or the rule of law had been fully established within them. It charged into the Euro, failed to implement that new currency's own rules and saw populist revolts overwhelm the measures required to force economic convergence through austerity. It has tried to create a feeling of European citizenship decades before a real European consciousness has had time to develop. Its Parliament is cumbersome and relatively weak, its bureaucracy over-mighty and inflexible, its treaty-making astonishingly slow.

But, and it's a very important but, it is the only continent we have. That's not a matter of choice. Moreover, when the first Referendum was fought in 1975, the EEC represented only half of Europe. Fascistic Greece, Spain and Portugal were outside, as was Russian-occupied Eastern and Central Europe, as was Scandinavia. Rejecting the EEC would have been to turn our backs on the core countries of Europe but not on the continent itself.

Today, the story is different. With the exception of oil-fuelled Norway and money-filled Switzerland, almost every meaningful, large-scale European country is in the EU or desperately trying to join. To all intents and purposes, leaving the EU is absolutely the same as trying to leave Europe as a whole.

And yet, as we have seen, leaving is not actually possible. Geography says so. Leaving the EU isn't a clean divorce; it is like divorcing your partner and then having to live in their spare room for the rest of eternity; still subject to their house rules, still passing them on the stairs every day, but with no say in how the house is run.

We would not be out – we'd be half-in and half-out, tied to Europe by our location but trying hard to pretend we were not; a fantasy as stupid as it is dangerous, a road to nowhere, a triumph of ideology over pragmatism – exactly the opposite of what has driven Tory success for the past century.

What is more, in trying to square an impossible circle, the Conservative Party is losing its reputation for basic competence, its other great electoral strength of the past 50 or more years. Not everyone in the UK loved the entirety of Thatcher's (or Major's or Cameron's) policies but at least they knew that Conservative administrations were practical, economically savvy and willing to learn lessons from experiments which went wrong. Labour was seen as hopeless in actually governing, whether this arose from the example of bankrupt or corrupt local councils or even well-meaning plans that were just ineptly implemented (like the Blairite attempt to introduce competitive tendering for hospital cleaning, without adding adequate cleanliness standards, which contributed to the rise of MRSA in British hospitals).

It is, indeed, part of the long-term Conservative "offer" to the voters of Britain that a Tory government is a safe, if sometimes unloved, pair of hands.

Under the May administrations, that has gone out of the window. Ministers fall out of the administration almost weekly, either due to scandals, policy disagreements or ineptitude; ministers attack each other and backbenchers lay into each other with ever-increasing ferocity; policies are decided and undecided at the drop of a hat (or rather the growling of an extremist Brexiteer) and meanwhile all the vital questions facing the country on housing, education, defence, the NHS etc are pushed into the background as the government blindly pursues a Hard Brexit policy for which there is no majority in the country, in Parliament or among Conservative voters. The CBI (albeit briefly) applauded Corbyn; businesses are threatening to up and leave, bankers (and their big tax payments) are relocating to Frankfurt, Paris, Amsterdam and Dublin; the armed forces and police are warning that they can no longer defend the British people…..and still the administration ploughs on as though nothing is happening while the wheels come off Great Britain Limited. It is just astonishing.

Can it be stopped and if so, how? What is the genuinely Conservative course of action? Is there a path out of the abyss?

11. A truly Tory U-turn

In today's era of quick soundbites and online news snippets, any complexity is unwelcome. Voters want to know where their leaders stand and demand simple, indeed simplistic, answers to some very complex questions. With all too many citizens unwilling to embrace the complexity and nuances of the real world or to hear views which challenge their prejudices, they are falling into the trap of self-reinforcing circles, getting a continuous feedback loop from Facebook or Twitter of views which accord with their own. That is comforting for them – but it is also very dangerous for any society.

With regard to the Brexit debate, these trends have undoubtedly had the effect of hardening the positions of both sides. That makes it far, far harder for the leaders of the Brexiteers to admit that maybe they got it wrong – that Brexit is not simple, or profitable, that it doesn't take back control, that it will not give us £350 million per week for the NHS (or anything else) – and that it is not a policy for true Conservatives.

For them to row back from where they currently sit will be hard, but a look back at the Conservative Party and its great leaders should give them considerable succour.

Anyone not studying history would be forgiven for thinking that the best Tory party leaders were all engrained with loyal Conservative sympathies from the cradle to the grave – that they were the true carriers of the flame.

The reality is quite different. Almost every outstanding Tory leader was, at some point, something else – and indeed, many great leaders of other Parties started out as, or later became, Conservatives.

The two Pitts, for example, would have thought of themselves as Whigs (the eighteenth century opposition to the Tories) up until the French revolution; Peel, the creator of the modern Conservative Party, was expelled from it after repealing the Corn Laws in 1846; with him went Gladstone, and they created the Peelites, who eventually merged with the Whigs to form the modern Liberal Party. Similarly, Palmerston, the greatest Whig Prime minister, had started life as a Tory (and was surely one of the most conservative leaders the country has ever had). Moving in the opposite direction was Disraeli, who first stood as a Radical before signing up to the Tory ranks, a similar journey to Joseph Chamberlain's. Moving to the 20th century, the most famous example of crossing the benches is Churchill, who went from the Tories to the Liberals and back again; and then, having been shunned by Conservative backbenchers, was propelled to power by a National coalition, cheered on by Labour and Liberal MPs to the stony silence of the majority of elected Conservatives. More recently as we know, Tony Blair tried to join the Conservatives at university,

CHAPTER 11

before being put off and deciding to join Labour and remove the socialist sting from it.

If most of the greatest leaders in the Conservative Party's history have been willing to change their colours and their policies, what about the Party itself? Has it, too, adopted flagship policies, only to reverse them when they did not seem workable in practice.

The answer is a resounding "yes".

Indeed, the entire history of the Tory and Conservative Parties resonates with the sound of reversing engines. In the eighteenth century, many Tories were sympathetic to a Jacobite restoration and even to armed rebellion. That went nowhere. In the nineteenth century, the Party opposed Catholic Emancipation (the right of Catholics to vote and hold public office) only to enact it under the great Duke of Wellington; supported the Corn Laws (protectionist tariffs which kept the price of grain high to the benefit of farmers and the landowning aristocracy) only to repeal them; opposed extension of the franchise, only the pass the largest such measure to date in 1867; and opposed trade unions, only to legalise them. In the 20th century, it brought in imperial preference (essentially a Customs Union for the Empire) only to revert to free trade and of course wholeheartedly embraced appeasement, which only a tiny minority of Conservative MPs challenged, right up until Hitler's occupation of Czechoslovakia. Many of us will remember defending the poll tax on the doorsteps in the 1987 general election, only for it to be abandoned in the light of massive civil (and some extremely uncivil) disobedience under the Major government. It was that abandonment of an unworkable manifesto commitment which won the 1992 election for the Conservatives.

This trend of periodic U-turns has all been framed by the Party's unflinching desire for power, usually justified on the basis of moderating a current trend which Conservatives dislike and from which they wish to defend the country, but with a willingness to accept and move on where the spirit of the age is against them.

It is rare, indeed, for the Conservative party to cling to a policy when the facts on the ground show it to be unworkable. Perhaps the best example from among the situations outlined above is the repeal of the Corn Laws in 1846. Robert Peel, who had fashioned the new Conservative Party out of the ruins of the defeated Tories in the 1830s, had won the 1841 election determined to uphold such laws. It was a central plank of his manifesto in an age when the landed aristocracy still controlled many seats. However, the famine in Ireland, exacerbated by the shortage of cheap corn to make up for the failure of the potato crop on that island, showed Peel that the policy was indefensible both morally and in terms of increasing the wellbeing of the overall population (and so supporting the nation's fighting strength) – an utter disaster at every level.

Peel did the right thing. He put country before party and, as a result, lost his job, with the bulk of his ministers splitting off to form a Peelite Party (with most eventually morphing into Liberals) while the remaining hard-core protectionists held onto the mantle of the Conservative Party – and were out of power for most of the next 28 years, earning the mocking title of "the Stupid Party". (If there's a lesson in history for the Conservative Party of today, here it surely lies!)

Moreover, it is worth noting that the Peelite rebels went on to run Britain for most of the 30 years after 1846 – just as the anti-appeasement rebels in the form of Churchill, Eden and Macmillan ran the Tory party from 1940 to the 1960s. Those on the wrong side of history lost both their honour and their chances of power.

The basic message from all this history is that when a policy – however passionately believed in by the party's activists, however firmly embedded in the manifesto – is clearly damaging to the country, the Conservative Party has usually been willing to rethink it when faced with the obligations of governing. That is why we have a system of representative government where MPs have the final say, not a system of power delegated by referenda or "people's committees".

Today, we need to see that same sense of responsibility from our MPs. We have, in Theresa May, a prime minister who seems to want to mimic Lord Liverpool the Tory PM from 1812 to 1827 who owed his longevity in office to continually kicking the can down the road, avoiding dealing with parliamentary reform or Catholic Emancipation for so long that when those issues exploded, they took the party down.

Since then, the hallmark of Conservative administrations has generally been a pragmatic determination to tackle the real problems facing Britain and to do so without fear or favour. What made so many voters turn to Margaret Thatcher was her willingness to put the party at risk to do what was right for Britain – in contrast to our current PM who seems quite willing to put Britain at risk for the sake of the party.

It is not only Maggie though. Pitt the Younger split from the old Whigs to stand firm against the French revolution; Peel as we have seen, put righting the ills of the poor ahead of the interests of his government; Churchill endured years of opprobrium for his opposition to appeasement. The bravest and best Conservative leaders are those who put Britain first.

As this tome should have made clear, there are many ills threatening the country – creaking public services, a huge government deficit, stagnating living standards, weakened police and armed forces in an increasingly dangerous world, the danger of Scotland and Northern Ireland breaking away from the UK, significant immigration both legal and illegal, and the long-term rise of the Asian economies in competition with those of Europe and America.

The answer to those dilemmas is not Brexit. Instead, the Conservative Party should rally around the policy supported by every serving Conservative Prime Minister since the days of Macmillan. It is to engage with Europe and, where possible, to lead it. To make sure that our continent does, as far as possible, what we want it to do; that it acts as our robotic arm, strengthening and projecting our power and our policies intro the world from a position of strength.

Ironically, given how she is revered by the Brexiteers, it is Margaret Thatcher's administrations which show us the way. They first addressed the unfairness of the EU budget, where we were continuing massively to prop up inefficient French farmers through the Common Agricultural Policy – they secured the UK rebate, still in place (but probably gone for ever if we leave and tried to rejoin later). Then they tackled the massive problem of non-tariff barriers which allowed other EU countries to frustrate British exporters of good and services even within the Customs Union. We won a resounding victory allowing the creation of the Single Market. Finally, her governments pressed to lock in the countries of Eastern Europe to the EU, to ensure they could not fall back into the orbit of Russia, a policy which also met remarkable success, at least until the last few years.

What the Conservative Party in this era recognised is that if "Europe" is inevitable, which it is, then the UK is far better off in the driving seat, not the back seat and definitely not being thrown out of the car entirely into the dusty road.

We won the game by playing it, not by running away. We won because British pragmatism usually beats continental flights of fancy. We won by being confident, proud and assertive, a Churchillian Britain thrusting forwards, not a Chamberlainite Little England skulking in the corner.

Conservatives can return to that, but to do so, we must take back control of our party. It will not be easy. There is a fight ahead. The purveyors of Project Scare will call us "enemies of the people" – just as they have branded the Lords, the judges and presumably, since a majority of Britons currently want to stay in the EU, the people themselves, as "enemies of the people".

True Tories must not be cowed by the loud mouths of the extremists, whether in Parliament, in Conservative associations around Britain or in Australian and Canadian owned newspapers.

Nor must they be lured by the siren voices within the Conservative Party calling for a "compromise solution" which is a bit like saying "we'll drive over the cliff but only fall half way down" as though that were possible. Being a rule-taker not a rule-maker in our own Continent may suit Switzerland, Norway, Iceland or Liechtenstein – it is not the right place for a great nation like ours.

So, what to do? With events moving so fast, it is impossible to set out a real programme. It may be that we get no deal with the EU at all. Certainly, the current

British position would indeed produce a "cake and eat it" result, which might encourage other EU countries to follow the UK out of the door. That is an existential threat to the EU which it will not accept; and the EU's ability to survive a "no deal" scenario is significantly better than the UK's.

Alternatively, given the very short-time-frame, the PM may come back with a half-cut deal, to be fully negotiated during a transition period. That would – and should – be difficult for Parliament to accept because it is a bridge without a destination.

Or she may accept the ultimate logic of her position on Northern Ireland – already agreed with the EU remember – and keep the UK effectively in the Single Market, braving the inevitable challenge from the hardliners.

Whatever comes back, it is highly likely that it will be worse, by far, than what the UK enjoys now.

That will be the time for Conservative Remainers both inside and outside Parliament to find their voice, whether by voting down a deal and taking over the negotiation; insisting on a free vote of MPs or maybe even calling for a popular vote as to whether to take the deal or abandon Brexit as a lost cause.

Which of these routes to take will be difficult to decide. Theresa May, if she has not been toppled, will want to just keep fudging – she may even back the idea of asking the EU to extend the Article 50 process by pushing back the deadline of 29th March 2019. The

EU as a body might decide to agree such an extension to the Article 50 process but it requires the support of all 27 other countries for this to be enacted. So, for example, Ireland is in a prime position to put some conditions on an extension – as might other countries (like Spain with regard to loyal Gibraltar, which the Brexiteers are also happy to throw to the wolves). If Ireland's conditions include "no hard border" as they might well, we are back to square one, with the need to produce a solution which is not only workable, but which Ireland and the rest of the EU also accept as being workable, something not yet achieved.

Moreover, it is hard to see Parliament agreeing to any deal which May is able to produce. If it involves accepting reality, the Brextremists may rebel; if it does not, the Conservative pro-Europeans will rebel and almost certainly in greater numbers than they have shown to date.

As the former Education Secretary, Justine Greening, has recognised, for an issue which cuts so strongly across party lines, the logical solution would be a free vote; and yet for that very reason it is unlikely to be accepted by either May or Corbyn.

In the end, though, it may be that the only way for politicians to escape from the mess they have created will be to put it back to the people – just as David Cameron did in 2016. It is, quite frankly, a total indictment of Britain's political class that this might need to happen again; and referenda are miles away from being the policy instrument of Burkean Conservatives or indeed Thatcherite ones, that lady having called them a "device of dictators and demagogues". However, if it is the only option left, it may be the option we need to take.

Even then, to get a People's Vote will require Parliament to vote for it. That will necessitate courage from the moderates, of which too many of them have so far shown little. Partly that's because they have become prisoners of the "will of the people" myth and, before this tome closes, that is something which has to be addressed. However much we, as Conservatives, may dislike referenda and regard them as populist instruments beloved of unscrupulous dictators; however much we may recognise that people often vote in them based on a wide range of emotions that have nothing to do with the question on the ballot paper; we also have to recognise that a Tory government called one and promised to honour it. However true it may be – and it *is* true – that it was constitutionally non-binding, can we just toss it aside? We'd better have a pretty good reason for doing so. Do we?

Fortunately, we do. It is a painful British quirk that we hate to moan, to be bad losers; as a result, the Remoaner label is one that pro-EU politicians have allowed to stick rather than challenging it openly; the Brexiteers have, as usual, won a propaganda battle which portrays any politician questioning what happened in May and June 2016 as somehow undemocratic.

That ignores another very British character trait – the

desire for fair play; because what it very clear, and becoming clearer all the time, is that the 2016 Referendum, far from being the greatest democratic exercise in the history of the United Kingdom, was actually the greatest travesty of democracy the country has ever seen, at least in the modern era.

Why? Let's consider all the ways in which the Referendum was badly conducted:

a) Basic Honesty

While politicians have been widely distrusted by the population at large for a long time, we have – until recently – always maintained at least some level of integrity in the political discourse in the UK. For sure, during every election campaign, one minister or shadow minister will get a fact completely wrong or fail to remember a crucial statistic – perhaps unimpressive, but rarely showing outright mendacity. Equally, at election times, each party tries to paint its rival in the worst possible light – "Labour will destroy our defences", "the Tories will privatise the NHS" etc. These may be malicious claims but, as forward-looking statements, they can arguably be accepted as misguided fears rather than outright lies. We saw some of this behaviour during May and June 2016 i.e. politicians misleading the public but not telling outright porkies. We were told by Leavers, as discussed earlier, that the post-Brexit deal would be easy and that the EU needed us more than we need them; we were told by Brexiteers that immigration would be brought under control quickly and easily after Brexit, something which the Leave camp then reversed within two days of winning the vote. Equally, the Chancellor of the Exchequer took the most favourable (from his perspective) end of the many independent forecasts which were published during the campaign, on all aspects of a post-Brexit economy. To make it worse, the Remain campaign said at one and the same time that Brexit was a leap into the unknown and that it was bound to be a disaster in all conceivable scenarios, which two points are hard to square logically.

All just a bit dodgy, to be sure…..but not the same as bare-faced lying.

Unfortunately, this Referendum campaign brought us something completely different – supposedly serious politicians telling outright factual lies and, indeed, making them the centrepiece of a campaign. These could have been nuanced so as not to be lies, for example, "one day Turkey may join the EU" or "the UK's gross budget contribution is £350 million". Could have been, but were not. Instead, we were told that Turkey's accession was imminent and that the UK had no veto over it; we were told that £350 million per week was all coming back, ready to be deployed into the NHS (and at the same time given to farmers, impoverished regions, projects to create tighter border controls etc). Maybe I was just unlucky, but the only two Leave leaflets that came through my front door were on these two topics. I am sure I was not alone.

"Why all the fuss?" ask most politicians when confronted with this – even pro-Remain Conservative MPs. The "fuss" is about the most basic imperative of any democracy – that of offering voters a range of genuine choices. While the world of politics does not seem to understand this, the worlds of finance, business and commerce do. Advertisements must be "decent, honest and truthful" and there is an authority to monitor that. Banks and insurance companies can be (and have been) fined billions of pounds for mis-selling financial products. Shoppers have consumer protection, which means shops have to show prices accurately, take back faulty goods and display price comparisons fairly. In short, a businessperson selling you something can be held to account if they lie; a politician selling their country down the river can get away with it scot-free. Witness the astonishing (if short-lived) rehabilitation of Boris Johnson who lied about how the country spends its money; compare that to the impeachment of Dilma Rousseff in Brazil for doing the same thing and weep.

b) Following the rules of the game

We knew immediately that the Leave campaigns had lied – but it took longer for the word to emerge that they had also cheated, overspending their limits considerably and covering it up. However, in July 2018, the Electoral Commission reported that Vote Leave had co-ordinated its campaign with another group, BeLeave and, together, they had overspent the £7 million campaign allowance by £500,000.

According to the Electoral Commission, Vote Leave also did its best to hamper the investigation: Bob Posner, of the Electoral Commission, also criticised the campaign, saying Vote Leave had:

> ... *resisted our investigation from the start, including contesting our right as the statutory regulator to open the investigation ... It has refused to cooperate, refused our requests to put forward a representative for interview, and forced us to use our legal powers to compel it to provide evidence. Nevertheless, the evidence we have found is clear and substantial, and can now be seen in our report. [The commission found] serious breaches of the laws put in place by parliament to ensure fairness and transparency at elections and referendums.*[47]

Before we continue, we have to ask whether a bit of lying and cheating matters very much and I would have respond that, as a Conservative, I think it matters a great deal on several levels:

> I. Because, as Conservatives, we are supposed to be upholders of our constitution and it is undermined if we allow people to break its rules. If you argue that the lying did not matter then the question has to arise: at what point *does* dishonesty matter – or do you accept any and all of it, as Trump expects Americans to do?

> II. Because, as Conservatives, we are supposed to be the party which tells it "as it is", asking people

to face difficult truths. That was what the Thatcher revolution was based on – "if it isn't hurting, it isn't working". If we are now the party which lies as a matter of convenience, we are losing our soul.

III. In the case of the Referendum it also matters because the result was close. If you win with 52% of the vote, the fact that you may have overspent your campaign by 7.1% is relevant; the fact that you put falsehoods as the main campaigning themes matters a lot. Simply put, if Leave had not lied and cheated they would probably have lost. The dishonesty changed the course of British history – and that's not all right.

If they were the only things wrong with the Referendum that would be bad enough. However, it was also skewed in many ways to favour a Leave vote:

c) The Franchise was messed up

That sounds a pretty boring topics doesn't it? I mean we all know how it works – if you are British and over 18 you get to vote and if not, you do not right? Actually, no.

Firstly, expats living abroad for more than 15 years have lost that right. Perhaps that is acceptable because if you've really gone away for good, why should you decide the fate of the rest of us? Except that people who moved to other EU countries were told that they were living in a single community with shared rights. What is more the 2015 Conservative manifesto promised to restore their votes – and we then went back on it.

Secondly, Commonwealth citizens who had lived in the UK for six months were also able to vote. Even a Rwandan (a country we never colonised but decided to join the Commonwealth) could, on that basis, have decided our European future.

At the same time, thirdly, no EU passport holders (except for Irish citizens) had the right to vote in the Referendum. Not if they have lived in the country for 30 years; not even if they were married to a Brit. In normal circumstances, fair enough – but, as with British expats, these were people who were happy to live in the UK under EU rules and the concept of a shared set of rights. Many failed to apply for British citizenship because they did not need to as EU citizens; but may now lose those rights based on a vote from which they were excluded.

In a close vote, these rules may have made a lot of difference, unfairly in all cases, and if we vote again they should be changed.

Of course, all of these points, however valid they undoubtedly are, sound like a Remoaner manifesto – things you complain about if you have lost. For neutrals in the debate, they may not sound convincing; just an attempt to re-open the decision.

Fortunately, they are only a part of the overall discussion. There are other, even more compelling, reasons

BREXIT – A BETRAYAL OF CONSERVATISM?

to challenge the need to be locked into a "will of the people" mandate from more than two years ago:

1) The question asked of "the people" gave no direction. Asking people if they want to Remain in a reformed EU or leave it, is a bit like asking somebody "would you like to sell your house"? It is a valid question in and of itself, but – as we are discovering daily – it is only half of a question. It provides no clue at all as to destination. "Would you like to sell your house and by the way, you can get this mansion in the Bahamas really cheaply" is a rather different question from "Would you like to sell your house and live on a rubbish tip?".

As a result of asking only half a question, politicians can make up whatever answer they wish to the second half. Brexiteers argue that Leave voters "must have" wanted to leave the Single Market and Customs Union but there is no evidence of that at all. Actually, polls consistently show a majority for remaining in them. As to the idea that voters consciously decided to leave ECJ jurisdiction that suggests a far higher level of knowledge of the intricacies of the EU's working than exists. Even some MPs on the Leave side do not seem to know the difference between the ECJ (the EU's court for enforcing its rules) and the European Court of Human Rights (which is governed by the Council of Europe and nothing to do with the EU) so it's hardly fair to expect the bulk of voters to have done so.

CHAPTER 11

2) The Brexit we are getting is not the Brexit we were promised. As we know, many promises were made during the Referendum. Some Brexiteers promised a clean break, with no ties to the EU at all. Others promised that we would be able to have "friction-free" access to EU markets. Indeed, for the most part voters were offered the two together – an easy deal where we got *both* friction-free access and complete freedom.

Anyone now looking at the total dog's breakfast currently on offer can see that the "real deal" is not what was promised at the time they voted. They were sold on a false prospectus and if that makes Brexit sound like a financial deal, it is in fact from business that we can see how to proceed. In business, when you buy a company, the process usually works as follows. The buyer makes on offer and, if the seller likes it, they give the buyer a period to do "due diligence" i.e. an extensive checking that what the seller had told the buyer is fully accurate. If, in doing your due diligence, you find that the target company is not the same as had been claimed, you can walk away or reduce your price. It is much the same when you buy a home in England – you do a local authority search, do a survey, check the title deeds etc. If something is wrong, you don't have to complete. The same applies again if you are looking to buy a car; you are able to have a test drive first to see if it lives up to expectations. For patients facing an operation, once again, there is a need to understand what they are letting themselves in for – a process requiring what is termed "informed consent" whereby the patient must sign a form confirming they comprehend the procedures and risks. In simple terms, with almost all significant activities which people undertake today, they are protected by the right to know the facts before they have to sign on the dotted line.

We are in a similar procedure today with Brexit but that fundamental right to "review and rethink" is being denied to the British people on the most important political decision of our era.

We were offered various types of Brexit in 2016 but the choice on offer today is fundamentally different.

The choice Theresa May is offering is that we can crash out with no deal, not get friction-free trade, not safeguard the right of UK expats on the Continent and be at the mercy of any other potential trade partners with whom we try to negotiate. Or we can secure friction-free trade with the EU by allowing free movement to continue and paying into the EU budget. The third option, the one currently being withheld from us, is to decide to stay as we are – which is what most companies and house buyers do if they find that whet they are likely to get is very different from what they were first offered.

The moral case for allowing people to step back from the brink is overwhelming.

At the same time, politicians are astonishingly reluctant to lead on this. Unlike the Peels, Churchills and Thatchers of the past, today's politicians prefer to follow public opinion and to bend their views to those of the focus groups. Real leadership is largely absent and when you see it, all too often it comes from fanatics.

However for our nervous political class, even on the grounds of "they are my leaders, I must follow them", there is overwhelming evidence that the people have a right to change their minds.....because they *have* changed their minds! In a significant majority of opinion polls conducted over the past 12 months, Remain has led Leave. That is actually quite remarkable given that (i) neither the Tory nor the Labour leadership, nor indeed even the pro-EU Tory or Labour rebels has made the case for Remaining and (ii) the Brexiteers are very good at painting the EU as an evil "mafia" when it will not concede to their demands. Indeed, when faced with a choice of a "no deal" Brexit or Remaining, in a You Gov poll on 16/17th July 2018, voters backed Remaining by 55% to 45%. The "Will of the People", as at mid-2018, is to stay in the EU.[48]

The case for a new popular vote is therefore absolutely compelling:

> 1) The original vote was flawed in conception and practice – in the franchise, in the question asked and the way it was conducted, with no material sanction at all against Leave's dishonesty

2) The Brexit we are ending up with doesn't look at all like what we were promised – it is worse in all material respects

3) The people now favour remaining in the EU – why should a decision taken over two years ago, which the voters now realise was the wrong decision, be forced on an unwilling country, especially when perhaps two million elderly (mostly Leave) voters have passed away and been replaced on the electoral roll by a similar number of younger voters who are overwhelmingly Remainers. Do the votes of the dead outweigh the votes of the living?

However, if we get that new popular vote, we will need a centre-right voice to be explaining why Brexit isn't pure Toryism – it is the absolute opposite, as this book explains. In other words, we need our MPs to put country before party, and honour ahead of career. They need to remember what it means to be a Conservative and to take the path forward on Brexit which is unquestionably the correct one.

The right course, the Conservative course, the patriotic course, is to remain in the EU. It is a fact, not an option.

References

[1] Opinium, 2018. *Political Polling 10th July 2018.* [online]. Available at: https://www.opinium.co.uk/political-polling-10th-july-2018-3 [Accessed 25 August 2018].

[2] Watts, J., 2018. Brexit: Most Conservative voters who backed Theresa May in 2017 would favour second referendum. *Independent*, [online]. Available at: https://www.independent.co.uk/news/uk/politics/conservatives-poll-second-brexit-referendum-spring-conference-survation-theresa-may-a8259966.html [Accessed 25 August 2018].

[3] Shipman, T., 2016. *All Out War: The Full Story of How Brexit Sank Britain's Political Class* (p. 617). London: HarperCollins.

[4] Porter, A. (ed.), 1999. *The Oxford History of the British Empire: Volume III: The Nineteenth Century* (p. 35). Oxford: Oxford University Press.

[5] Pope, R. (ed.), 1989. *Atlas of British Economic and Social History Since c.1700* (p. 107). London: Routledge.

[6] House of Commons Library, 2012. *UK trade statistics.* [pdf] House of Commons Library. Available at: http://researchbriefings.files.parliament.uk/documents/SN06211/SN06211.pdf [Accessed 25 August 2018].

[7] Trading Economics, 2018. *United Kingdom Exports By Country.* [online]. Available at: https://tradingeconomics.com/united-kingdom/exports-by-country [Accessed 25 August 2018].

[8] MacMillan, M., 2013. *The War That Ended Peace* (p.36). London: Profile Books Ltd.

[9] The Bruges Group, 2014. *Someone had Blunder'd.* [video online]. Available at: https://www.youtube.com/watch?v=hUq-N8GXvCA [Accessed 26 August 2018].

[10] Lester, N., 2018. A fifth of British troops are too unfit to fight, warns former Armed Forces chief. *Sunday Express*, [online] Available at: https://www.express.co.uk/news/uk/923677/British-Army-former-Armed-Forces-chief-warns-fifth-troops-too-unfit-action [Accessed 26 August 2018].

[11] Kennedy, P., 1989. *The Rise and Fall of the Great Powers.* London: Fontana.

[12] Busby, E., 2016. Exclusive new survey shows clear majority of teachers want to remain in the EU. *Times Educational Supplement*, [online]. Available at: https://www.tes.com/news/school-news/breaking-news/exclusive-new-survey-shows-clear-majority-teachers-want-remain-eu> [Accessed 26 August 2018].

[13] Morgan, J., 2016. EU referendum: nine out of 10 university staff back Remain. *Times Higher Education*, [online]. Available at: https://www.timeshighereducation.com/news/european-union-referendum-nine-out-of-ten-university-staff-back-remain [Accessed 26 August 2018].

[14] Clarke, P., 2016. The Brexit divide: How the City of London voted in the EU referendum. *eFinancialCareers*, [online]. Available at: https://news.efinancialcareers.com/uk-en/250125/this-is-how-city-of-london-workers-voted-in/ [Accessed 26 August 2018].

[15] [*Britain a mere province of the Common Market?*] 1975. [image online] Available at: https://flashbak.com/ephemera-from-the-1975-european-referendum-63088/ [Accessed 27 August 2018].

[16] ©: ZUMAPRESS.COM/Keystone Pictures USA/age footstock.

[17] Wikipedia, 2018. *Dispute settlement in the World Trade*

Organization. [online]. Available at: https://en.wikipedia.org/wiki/Dispute_settlement_in_the_World_Trade_Organization [As of 10 August 2018, 10:00 GMT].

[18] Full Fact, 2017. *Everything you might want to know about the UK's trade with the EU.* [online]. Available at: https://fullfact.org/europe/uk-eu-trade/ [Accessed 26 August 2018].

[19] Ibid.

[20] The Economist, 2018. After Brexit, which trade deals should negotiators prioritise? *The Economist*, [online] Available at: https://www.economist.com/britain/2018/02/08/after-brexit-which-trade-deals-should-negotiators-prioritise [Accessed 26 August 2018].

[21] Economics Online, 2018. *Gravity theory of trade.* [online]. Available at: http://www.economicsonline.co.uk/Global_economics/Gravity_theory_of_trade.html [Accessed 26 August 2018].

[22] Office of the United States Trade Representative, 2018. [online] Available at: https://ustr.gov/ [Accessed 28 August 2018].

[23] Trading Economics, 2018. *Germany Exports By Country.* [online]. Available at: https://tradingeconomics.com/germany/exports-by-country [Accessed 25 August 2018].

[24] Trading Economics, 2018. *United Kingdom Exports By Country.* [online]. Available at: https://tradingeconomics.com/united-kingdom/exports-by-country [Accessed 25 August 2018].

[25] Rachman, 2016. *Easternisation: War and Peace in the Asian Century* (p. 121). London: Vintage.

[26] Moore, F., 2016. Now meddling Australian PM says he would 'welcome' Britain staying in European Union. *Sunday Express*, [online]. Available at: https://www.express.co.uk/

news/uk/666221/malcolm-turnbull-eu-brexit-remain-australia-philip-hammond [Accessed 26 August 2018].

[27] McLain, S., 2016. India's Narendra Modi Weighs in Again on Brexit Debate. *The Wall Street Journal*, [online]. Available at: https://blogs.wsj.com/indiarealtime/2016/05/26/indias-narendra-modi-weighs-in-again-on-brexit-debate/ [Accessed 26 August 2018].

[28] The Guardian, 2016. Canada urges Britain to stay in the EU. *The Guardian*, [online]. Available at: https://www.theguardian.com/world/2016/may/19/brexit-canada-urges-britain-stay-eu-justin-trudeau [Accessed 26 August 2018].

[29] Office for National Statistics, 2018. *Employment by industry*. [online]. Available at: https://www.ons.gov.uk/employmentandlabourmarket/peopleinwork/employmentandemployeetypes/datasets/employmentbyindustry [Accessed 26 August 2018].

[30] Office for National Statistics, 2017. *Additional country data for trade in goods and services between 1999 and 2016*. [online]. Available at: https://www.ons.gov.uk/economy/nationalaccounts/balanceofpayments/adhocs/007716additionalcountrydatafortradeingoodsandservicesbetween1999and2016 [Accessed 26 August 2018].

[31] Cebr, 2016. *How the UK economy's key sectors link to the EU's single market*. [online]. Available at: https://cebr.com/reports/how-the-uk-economys-key-sectors-link-to-the-eus-single-market/ [Accessed 26 August 2018].

[32] Financial Times, 2017. 'Dark matter that matters' in UK trade with EU. *Financial Times*, [online]. Available at: https://www.ft.com/content/ceac2d00-dffc-11e7-a8a4-0a1e63a52f9c [Accessed 26 August 2018].

[33] OECD, 2018. *Foreign Direct Investment Statistics: Data, Analysis and Forecasts*. [online]. Available at: http://www.oecd.org/corporate/mne/statistics.htm [Accessed 27 August 2018].

34 UK public spending, 2018. *UK National Debt Analysis*. [online]. Available at: https://www.ukpublicspending.co.uk/uk_national_debt_analysis [Accessed 26 August 2018].

35 Office for National Statistics, 2018. *Economic well-being, UK: October to December 2017*. [online]. Available at: https://www.ons.gov.uk/peoplepopulationandcommunity/personalandhouseholdfinances/incomeandwealth/bulletins/economicwellbeing/octobertodecember2017 [Accessed 26 August 2018].

36 The World Bank, 2018. *Trade (% of GDP)*. [online]. Available at: https://data.worldbank.org/indicator/NE.TRD.GNFS.ZS [Accessed 26 August 2018].

37 The Guardian, 2018. Brexit blamed as record number of EU nurses give up on Britain. *The Guardian*, [online]. Available at: https://www.theguardian.com/society/2018/apr/25/brexit-blamed-record-number-eu-nurses-give-up-britain [Accessed 26 August 2018].

38 Office for National Statistics, 2018. *Migration Statistics Quarterly Report: August 2018*. [online]. Available at: https://www.ons.gov.uk/peoplepopulationandcommunity/populationandmigration/internationalmigration/bulletins/migrationstatisticsquarterlyreport/august2018 [Accessed 7 September 2018].

39 Times Higher Education, 2018. NHS crisis puts nurse training efforts in spotlight. *Times Higher Education*, [online]. Available at: https://www.timeshighereducation.com/news/nhs-crisis-puts-nurse-training-efforts-spotlight [Accessed 26 August 2018].

40 Bodkin, H., 2017. Near-record number of nurses start training despite drop in applicants. *The Telegraph*, [online]. Available at: https://www.telegraph.co.uk/news/2017/12/04/near-record-number-nurses-start-training-despite-drop-applicants/ [Accessed 26 August 2018].

41 London Economics, 2018. *The costs and benefits of*

international students by parliamentary constituency, [pdf] London: London Economics. Available at: http://www.hepi.ac.uk/wp-content/uploads/2018/01/Economic-benefits-of-international-students-by-constituency-Final-11-01-2018.pdf [Accessed 27 August 2018].

42 Oxford Economics, 2014. *The economic costs and benefits of international students*, [pdf] Oxford: Oxford Economics. Available at: https://www.sheffield.ac.uk/polopoly_fs/1.259052!/file/sheffield-international-studentsreport [Accessed 27 August 2018].

43 Scottish Government, 2018. European Structural and Investment Funds. [online]. Available at: https://beta.gov.scot/policies/european-structural-funds/ [Accessed 27 August 2018].

44 McKittrick, D., 2007. £1.5bn: annual cost of the enduring sectarianism in Northern Ireland. *Independent*, [online]. Available at: https://www.independent.co.uk/news/uk/this-britain/16315bn-annual-cost-of-the-enduring-sectarianism-in-northern-ireland-462649.html [Accessed 27 August 2018].

45 Crisp, J., 2018. EU ready to negotiate extradition treaty to replace European Arrest Warrant after Brexit. *The Telegraph*, [online]. Available at: https://www.telegraph.co.uk/politics/2018/05/25/eu-ready-negotiate-extradition-treaty-replace-european-arrest/ [Accessed 27 August 2018].

46 Towns, B., 2018. The Tories' Darkest Hour. *The New European*, [online]. Available at: https://www.theneweuropean.co.uk/top-stories/barnaby-towns-tories-darkest-hour-1-5419729 [Accessed 27 August 2018].

47 Elgot, J., 2018. Vote Leave fined and reported to police by Electoral Commission. *The Guardian*, [online]. Available at: https://www.theguardian.com/politics/2018/jul/17/vote-leave-fined-and-reported-to-police-by-electoral-commission-brexit [Accessed 26 August 2018].

[48] YouGov, 2018. *YouGov / The Times Survey Results*, [pdf]. Available at:

http://d25d2506sfb94s.cloudfront.net/cumulus_uploads/document/vv29cv0a94/TimesResults_SecondRef_180717_w.pdf [Accessed 26 August 2018].

Printed in Poland
by Amazon Fulfillment
Poland Sp. z o.o., Wrocław